50 Ways to Love Your Son

Approaching the Heart with a Rational Mind

Sarah Cline, Ph.D.

ISBN: 978-1-937209-25-4

Contents

Introduction

Welcome to *50 Ways to Love Your Son*. If you've picked up this book, you may be navigating familial challenges, eager to enhance existing familial bonds, or just gearing up for what the future holds in your family life. Whatever the case, you've taken a significant step toward deeper understanding and connection—so, congratulations are in order.

Throughout this volume and larger series, we'll focus on three universal personality categories: the reserved Cave Dweller (CD), the outgoing Mountain Yeller (MY), and the Straddler, who exhibits mixed traits. Recognizing and understanding these types is crucial, as they shape family dynamics in untold ways. Our aim is to provide practical insights into fundamental personalities, ensuring you're better equipped to navigate and strengthen your familial relationships. What's more, you'll walk away with a better grasp of who you truly are—and by knowing ourselves, you can offer more to your families.

Armed with the insights from this book, you'll not only interpret actions but also understand the deeper motivations behind them with greater ease. Prepare to see your son—and perhaps yourself—in a whole new light...

The Power of Personalities

Ahead, we'll demystify the core attributes of CDs, MYs, and Straddlers, equipping you with insights to comprehend and appreciate the nuances of each type. Appreciating these differences allows you to interpret your son's behaviors accurately within his unique personality context, thus avoiding flawed assumptions.

Too often in familial relationships, we mistakenly attribute conflicts and misunderstandings to a lack of love, empathy, or respect. Yet, more frequently, it's a simple gap in understanding. When you don't perceive the underlying personality traits driving your children's actions, you can misinterpret their intentions, leading to undue tension. It's not always about agreeing or having the same viewpoint; it's about acknowledging and respecting these inherent differences. By recognizing the core personality traits of CDs, MYs, and Straddlers, you can better empathize with your sons, allowing your bond to fully flourish.

Before We Begin

50 Ways to Love Your Son offers no quick fix or casual checklist. Instead, it emphasizes "love" as an active endeavor, demanding both attention and effort. While you'll find a great deal of guidance here, it's up to you to apply these insights authentically.

Engaging with this material will require introspection, and there will be moments that challenge your current understanding of parenting—and everything else. Yet, it's in these times of reflection and adjustment that true growth happens...and, here, the fruits of your labor could scarcely be sweeter—some real incentive.

Through patience and ongoing application, you're not just enhancing a single bond but, rather, refining how you connect. How you live. How you nurture his soul. So, cherish the process, love yourself, and love your son on a whole new level.

Before we begin, remind yourself: you're a masterpiece—and a work in progress.

Chapter One

Understanding Your Son's Personality Type

Do you find yourself struggling to understand your son's personality traits? Are you frustrated that they're so dissimilar to yours? Chances are, as your son grew, you embraced and enjoyed the differences he exhibited. But as he developed, those differences may have become sources of confusion or concern for you as a parent.

Understanding personality types is an essential piece of the puzzle when seeking to understand your son. Appreciating your child means discovering their many layers and complexities, and all of them should garner your attention if you are to foster a nurturing and understanding environment.

In this chapter, we will discuss the personality types of the Cave Dweller son, which we will refer to as CD, the Mountain Yeller, or MY son, and the Straddler son. Learning about these three basic personality types will give you a clearer picture of the unique benefits and challenges each creates. And understanding is an essential first step to bringing harmony and happiness into your everyday life.

Origins of Personality Types

Long before the modern-day classifications of CDs and MYs and even before psychiatrists and psychologists stepped onto the scene, ancient civilizations sought to explain human behavior and its various nuances.

The Ancient Greeks

The ancient Greeks developed the theory of "four humors" to explain the causes of health and illness, both mental and physical. This theory suggested that an individual's temperament was influenced by bodily fluids: blood (sanguine), yellow bile (choleric), black bile (melancholic), and phlegm (phlegmatic). The Greeks thought these humors were directly related to being sanguine (cheerful), choleric (short-tempered), melancholic (reserved), or phlegmatic (relaxed). Therefore, the balance of these humors was believed to influence an individual's temperament, health, and overall disposition. On the other hand, an imbalance of these humors led to behaviors that, today, we associate with certain mental illnesses. For example:

- Sanguine (blood) was associated with cheerful, optimistic, enthusiastic personality traits. An imbalance was thought to be due to a person having too much blood in their body, which would cause a person to be overly confident and have impulsive behavior. Possible narcissistic and/or bipolar disorder.

- Choleric (yellow bile) was associated with being ambitious, passionate, and easily angered. An imbalance causes anger, irritability, or extremely aggressive behavior and rage. Possible borderline personality disorder.

- Melancholic (black bile) was associated with being thoughtful, reflective, and often sad or depressed. This imbalance was associated with melancholy and depression.

- Phlegmatic (phlegm) was associated with being calm, reliable, and often unemotional or apathetic. An imbalance was associated with lethargy, sluggishness, or a lack of motivation, which, much like melancholic excess, is a symptom of depression.

Treating these emotional ailments is where things got even more interesting. If the Greeks thought you had an imbalance of any of these four humors, you would likely have received one of the following treatments:

Dietary Changes: Prescribed depending on the humor in excess. For instance, someone deemed overly choleric might be advised to avoid hot or spicy foods that would "agitate" the yellow bile.

Bloodletting: If you were someone believed to have an excess of sanguine humor, it was common practice to be prescribed bloodletting. This process involved removing blood from the body by way of leeches or actual cutting.

Purging: In order to remove excess bile or phlegm, laxatives were used, as were emetics, which induced vomiting.

Baths/Sweating: To promote toxin removal, balms and ointments were applied to the skin to help with the imbalance of any of these four humors.

The Greeks' attempts to "treat" imbalances in personality or health were based on the observations and the knowledge they had at the time. The four humors theory was eventually replaced with more

accurate medical models, but its influence can still be seen in some of
our languages today.

The Introvert and the Extrovert

Carl Gustav Jung (1875–1961) was a Swiss psychiatrist,
psychoanalyst, and the father of analytical psychology. He developed
several concepts that had a profound influence on both psychology
and popular culture. One of his most notable contributions was the
concept of "introversion" and "extraversion" (often used in the more
modern manner: introvert and extrovert). Jung's theory asserts that
introversion and extraversion are attitudes that represent the direction
in which a person's psychic energy flows.

Extraversion (Extrovert)

According to Jung, the extrovert's energy flows outward. This
personality type is more oriented toward the external world and
derives energy from interacting with its surroundings, including
people, events, and situations. If your son is an extrovert, he tends to be
more outgoing, social, and interested in external events. He is typically
action-oriented and is generally more comfortable in social situations
than an introverted man. Many extroverts are highly influenced by
external factors and are occasionally prone to negative introspection.

Introversion (Introvert)

As the name suggests, the introvert's energy flows inward. This
personality type is more oriented toward his inner world, relying
on introspection and internal reflection. If your son is introverted,
he is generally more reserved and often feels more comfortable with
individual activities or smaller group settings. He derives energy and

pleasure from thinking, daydreaming, or exploring ideas. Although an introvert's daily practices tend to lead to social isolation, many have a small number of deep connections with people of their choosing.

Jung believed that everyone has an introverted and extroverted side, with one being more dominant than the other. It's a spectrum, and while some might be near the extremes of that spectrum, most individuals fall somewhere in between.

Cave Dweller (CD) and Mountain Yeller (MY) Men

While not strictly rooted in these historical contexts, the CD and MY classifications are evolved constructs reflecting the same human desire to understand ourselves and others in our world more deeply.

While our contemporary understanding of the CD and MY classifications doesn't stem directly from ancient Greek or Jungian theories, much like their historical counterparts, they are observed patterns in modern relationships. By identifying recurring patterns, you can forge tools to help you navigate and harmonize interpersonal interactions.

Cave Dweller (CD) Son

To determine whether you and your son fall into the CD or MY category, you must first learn about their traits.

Reserved Nature

If your son is a CD, he will predominantly showcase a calm and reserved demeanor. He is introspective and tends to hold his emotions close to his chest because he values his inner world and the sanctuary it provides. His reserved nature doesn't mean that he is indifferent or detached; it just means that he processes his emotions internally and over time.

For instance, after an argument, a CD son might choose to withdraw to process his feelings rather than immediately confront an issue. He does this because he typically feels uncomfortable with strife and needs time to work through his emotions and how to communicate his feelings.

Socially, a CD son is often found in quieter corners, engaging in deep conversation with one or two individuals rather than in the center of a party. In group discussions, a CD will offer insights only if specifically asked or if he feels strongly about a topic.

Logical Thinking and Literal Communication

A CD son leans more toward analytical and logical thinking. He makes decisions only after careful contemplation and weighing the pros and cons. He works hard to keep his emotions from clouding his judgment. This logical thinking manifests in his communication, as he will get right to the point without inserting emotions or using stories to embellish his point.

For example, if you discuss a film with a CD son, he will likely dissect plot points with impeccable logic and even point out strengths and weaknesses. But he often misses the emotional undertones of the movie. If you ask a CD if he liked the cake you brought for dessert, he might reply, "Yes," without diving into flowery descriptives.

It's important to note that a CD son may also get frustrated with an embellished story that doesn't immediately get to the point. It doesn't mean he doesn't want to hear the story or doesn't care what the person has to say; his brain is just geared toward immediate outcomes.

Need for Space

A CD son has an inherent need for both emotional and physical personal space. For him, requiring space is not about distancing himself from loved ones. It's about needing solitude to recharge and reflect.

CD sons enjoy reading books in a cozy nook or going for solitary walks. He may listen to music while doing chores instead of talking. This alone time is essential for a CD son, especially after a day filled with social interactions.

Singular Focus

A CD son has unparalleled concentration when engrossed in a task and prefers completing that task to his satisfaction before tackling another.

If you attempt to talk to a CD son while he's studying or sketching, for example, he may be so absorbed in what he's doing that you'll be tuned out. It's not that what you're saying is unimportant to him; it's just challenging for him to spread his focus on more than one thing at a time because he gives each item his full attention.

Social Preferences

Traditionally, if your son were labeled an introvert, many would also consider him antisocial. But that couldn't be farther from the truth. An introvert, or a CD son, just leans toward more intimate social interactions. Large gatherings can leave a CD son feeling overwhelmed and quickly drain his mental and emotional battery.

Emotional Processing

While CD sons might not outwardly express their emotions, they experience them deeply. However, their internal reflections may lead to a delay in their outward emotional expression. While CD sons may seem distant after an emotional confrontation, many need to process the interaction before they react. A CD son needs time to contemplate a disagreement, analyze the conversation, and figure out where things went wrong before he can move on to a resolution. This meditation is essential for a CD son's parents to understand; the more they push him to express himself, the more he will clam up in response.

Fears Regarding Loss of Security

Finally, if your son is a CD, he craves stability in his life. Driven by a sense of perfectionism, he might demonstrate caution in his decisions, often opting for paths with predictable outcomes and minimal risk. At times, this drive for perfection and achievement might see him prioritizing tasks like studies over spending quality time with family. This isn't due to a diminished affection but stems from an intrinsic need for accomplishment and security. The hierarchy of basic needs for a CD son is as follows:

- Educational/Career Aspirations.

- Personal Interests/Friends.

- Family/Close Relationships.

- Personal Time/Recreation.

The position of each need doesn't mean they don't love and value their family. It means that it's essential for a CD son to feel that he's cementing a foundation of achievement and security before he can give his full attention to the next set of needs.

Deeper Dive into the Mountain Yeller (MY) Son

If your son is an extrovert, chances are he's been called that more than once in his lifetime. Extroverts are typically known for being outgoing and the life of any party. But there's so much more to them than meets the eye.

Outgoing Nature/Group Socialization

An MY son is inherently outgoing. His energy thrives on interactions and being around people as often as possible. Instead of needing time alone to recharge, an MY son wants to be out and involved.

At a social event, MY sons will be the first to initiate games and dancing and will often bounce from person to person, catching up rather than focusing on one task at a time. Deep conversations are still on the table, but not at a social event. MY sons are usually the ones who rally their friends for a group outing over a weekend rather than sitting at home reading a book or watching TV. Even at school or in the workplace, MY sons love group projects and find collaborative brainstorming and teamwork exciting.

Emotion-Driven

MY sons are heart ruled because they lead with their intuition and emotions. Being ruled by their heart doesn't mean their decisions are devoid of logic, but their feelings heavily influence their reactions. MY sons can be emotional during arguments but are also the first to send a heartfelt message to a friend upon hearing they are having a rough time.

An MY son's emotions will show throughout his storytelling, so be patient when he tells you about an event or relays the plot to a movie. Chances are both will be full of details and embellishments.

Connection and Touch

MY sons crave genuine connections and physical touch. Whether a hug, a pat on the back, or simply holding hands. It reinforces their feeling of being connected. In a relationship, the MY man will crave physical affection and see it as a top priority over other needs—something we'll discuss in depth a bit later.

Dynamic Focus

The MY son is a natural multitasker. Instead of focusing on one task at a time, his attention shifts between assignments. He enjoys the energy he gets from juggling multiple things and often gets bored working on one project for an extended period. It can be common to find the MY son drifting off during a long presentation. He's busy thinking about weekend plans.

The MY son doesn't mind dealing with homework, but he'll work through it while watching television or listening to music. As for conversations, the MY son loves to chat, but don't be surprised if you find the MY son scrolling on his phone while talking with you. It's not that the MY son thinks what you have to say is unimportant. His mind simply runs at higher speeds, and he's more comfortable when processing more than one thing at a time.

Inferential Communication

The MY son often communicates using stories, anecdotes, and metaphors rather than getting straight to the point. He relies on indirect implications and expects others to infer meanings, which can confuse some who may not be familiar with his communication style.

During an argument, the parent of an MY son may find it hard to decipher what the MY son really wants, even if he feels he has told them directly. It's essential to have a middle ground where communication is concerned, especially if your son is an MY trying to get through to a CD. Their communication styles are very different.

Immediate Emotional Expression

Unlike their CD counterparts, MY sons are quick to express their emotions. They're an open book and rarely hesitate to share their feelings of joy and disappointment. This can be overwhelming for a CD who is uncomfortable with an emotional display.

One of the greatest fears the MY son faces is the fear of rejection. If an MY son has a CD parent, who usually pulls away at any sign of conflict, this can be a bone of contention. The MY son will take your withdrawal as a sign of personal rejection. It's important to communicate that you are not rejecting him and that you simply need time to wrap your head around and process the disagreement. Give the MY son verbal and physical affirmations whenever possible.

The hierarchy of basic needs for the MY son is as follows:

- Friendships/Peers.

- Family.

- Personal Interests/Hobbies.

- Educational/Career Aspirations.

If you are a CD and your son is an MY, don't panic; it doesn't mean you cannot have a strong bond. There are plenty of amazing and fulfilling relationships between opposites. It just means it will take time, work, and patience to learn one another's needs and effectively communicate.

The Straddler

If your son is a Straddler, he is adaptable and enjoys the best of both worlds. He can immerse himself in a book like a CD or be the life of a party like an MY. He possesses an emotional agility that allows him to straddle his personality types seamlessly. While this book predominantly focuses on CD and MY sons, Straddlers can use it to understand the extremes and navigate their middle ground more effectively.

Excellent Balance between Reflection and Expression

A Straddler son can introspect like a CD, valuing quiet moments of thought. Yet, he also appreciates the expressive vitality of the MY and shares his feelings and ideas openly when a situation calls for it. He is as happy spending a quiet evening reading as he is going to a book club and actively participating in a lively discussion.

Adaptable in Social Situations

While he might not always be the life of the party, he easily adjusts to situations based on the social settings and the company involved. He can engage in a one-on-one conversation at a party and then join a group game or be the center of the party later in the evening.

Values Both Logic and Emotion

A Straddler son approaches situations with a logical mindset but is equally attuned to the emotional undercurrents, valuing the importance of feelings in decision-making. For example, if a peer faces a personal issue, the Straddler son will offer practical solutions while simultaneously providing emotional support.

Flexibility in Needs and Fears

The Straddler son's hierarchy of needs will fluctuate based on circumstances, and he might experience fears from the CD's spectrum, such as loss of security, as well as the MY's fear of rejection. However, adaptability allows him to prioritize different aspects of his life. While working on an important school project, he will prioritize educational achievement, but in his downtime, he will focus on friendships and familial connections.

Fluid Communication Styles

A Straddler son can communicate both directly and inferentially, often adjusting his communication based on the recipient. For example, when conversing with a detail-oriented teacher, he will be direct and to the point, but when he talks to his best friend, he becomes expressive and delves into all the nitty-gritty details.

Straddlers possess an innate ability to mediate and find common ground, especially in scenarios where CDs and MYs might find themselves at odds. His adaptability enables him to comprehend and empathize with both personality types, easing communication and diminishing misunderstandings.

A Straddler son is highly adaptable. However, everyone encounters their share of struggles. The flexibility of a Straddler often causes confusion about his preferences and needs. He might sometimes feel stretched or trapped in the middle, particularly in a polarized situation where he wishes to please his parents or peers and struggles to voice his disagreements. A Straddler son must discern what is truly significant to him while also learning to relate to the diverse personalities around him, much like everyone else.

So, How Do You Find Common Ground?

I'm a CD, and my son is an MY; will we always be at odds?

Absolutely not! In this book, we don't tell you how to "cope" with your son's differences. Instead, we empower you to recognize the unique strengths each personality type possesses. A CD's introspection can balance an MY's spontaneity. An MY's vivacity and exuberance can harmonize beautifully with a CD's depth and stability.

Recognizing these different traits is merely the first step to fostering a strong bond. The real challenge, and indeed the focus of this book, is to find ways to navigate the complexities of these interactions. After all, the beauty of the parent-child relationship truly unfolds in the dance between these personalities.

Key Takeaways

Diving into the intricacies of personality types isn't about affixing labels but rather enriching our understanding. With these insights, you're now armed with the necessary vocabulary to navigate the labyrinth of human emotions and connections, fostering an environment where respect grows, comprehension deepens, and bonds strengthen. As you traverse this journey, let's remember that the goal isn't to change but to adapt, understand, and love more deeply.

The foundation for a nurturing bond starts with understanding—understanding yourself, your son, and the dynamics of your interaction. With the knowledge of CD and MY personality traits, you're well on your way to deepening that understanding, setting the stage for the subsequent chapters that will guide you on how to cherish your son in ways that resonate with both of you.

Understanding personality differences is essential for nurturing compatibility. This chapter has illuminated the fundamental traits of CDs, MYs, and Straddlers.

- **Express, Don't Explode:** When speaking to your son, articulate feelings carefully. Address issues directly, focusing on one topic at a time.

- **Listen and Hear:** Actively listening to your son means more than just catching his words. Engage deeply, decipher underlying feelings, and resonate with his emotions.

- **Narrate Neutrally:** Use "I" and "we" statements when discussing family matters. These phrases are more than just words; they pave the way for understanding without triggering defenses.

- **Pivot Your Approach:** Understand the value CDs place on silence for introspection, and amplify the natural vibrancy of MYs with affirming words.

- **Establish Clear Boundaries:** Set them. Honor them. If your son has boundaries differing from yours, embrace them. Engage in dialogues to find common ground.

- **Initiate Family Check-Ins:** Regular reflections on your bond with your son provide direction. Treat these moments as opportunities for growth, not confrontations. And when he seeks alone time, respect it—solitude is essential for personal insight.

- **Share, Grow, Connect:** Narrate personal stories of growth and challenges with your son. It's not just about sharing experiences—it's about intertwining your familial narratives.

The key is understanding and complementing each other's rhythms. When personalities harmonize through understanding and respect, relationships flourish.

Chapter Two

Communication Is Key

Communication is the cornerstone of any strong parent-child relationship. It's the vital link that helps you connect across distinct personality types. This chapter aims to guide you through the facets of effective communication, specifically tailored to understand and validate your son's needs and character.

While the idea that the parent-child bond comes naturally can be comforting, building a lasting relationship with your son demands intentional effort, mutual respect, and a genuine desire to understand. This involves going beyond superficial knowledge of his likes and dislikes; it requires you to engage deeply with his personality traits and understand how they mesh with your own.

In an era where instant messaging has overtaken heartfelt conversation, you must not lose sight of the power of authentic human connection. Patience, reflection, and presence are irreplaceable components of a strong bond. So, as you read through this chapter, you're encouraged to stop, think, and absorb. Open, respectful communication cultivates more than a functional relationship; it nurtures a thriving emotional connection between you and your son. Below are some key strategies to help you articulate your emotions effectively.

Express Feelings Effectively without Instigating Conflicts

Communication is a cornerstone in any relationship, but for expressing emotions to your son, the stakes are high. Emotional outbursts can strain the relationship, making it vital to tread carefully.

Stay Calm

It's easy to get carried away in the heat of the moment, but maintaining your composure is critical. Being calm encourages your son to lower his defenses and listen. To cultivate calmness, consider techniques like mindfulness or even a simple count of ten before speaking.

Use Words, Not Actions to Express Feelings

Anger and frustration are often easier to show than to explain. However, lashing out physically or through actions can be damaging. When the tension rises:

- Step outside and get some fresh air.

- Engage in a few minutes of focused breathing.

- Interact with a pet to ease tension.

- Journal your thoughts to process emotions.

- Dive into a chapter of a good book to divert your focus.

These are more than distractions; they're ways to gain perspective and approach the issue anew.

Be Direct and Focused

It can be tempting to speak in vague terms, especially when the subject is uncomfortable. However, generalized statements make it difficult for your son to understand what's wrong. Therefore, keep your communication clear and centered around the problem at hand.

Stick to the Present Topic

When emotions run high, it's easy to bring up past wrongdoings, giving rise to the "kitchen sink effect." American psychologist and professor at the University of Washington, Dr. John M. Gottman, coined the term. It refers to overwhelming conversations with unrelated past issues. Gottman's research on relationship dynamics reveals how this technique undermines productive dialogue. Doing this overloads your son emotionally and derails the main issue.

Navigating the Kitchen Sink Effect

When tension escalates, it's common to lapse into the unproductive habit of bringing up past issues—the "kitchen sink effect." Several underlying causes may lead you down this path:

- A frequent motivator for resorting to "kitchen sinking" is the simple, albeit misguided, urge to win the argument at any cost. This is a classic example of winning a battle but setting yourself up to lose the war. It erodes the trust and goodwill that are vital for any meaningful relationship.

- A deficit in communication skills is another likely culprit. Sometimes, you aren't even aware that you're torpedoing the conversation by dragging in past grievances, largely because you've never learned effective ways to deal with lingering emotional baggage.

The risk of bringing up the past is that it derails the conversation and leaves the original issue unresolved. When you get ready to recount history in an argument, it could be a sign that you're avoiding the actual problem.

Instead of opting for this roundabout way of dealing, strive for focused communication. Your goal isn't to outmaneuver your son in a verbal duel but to foster understanding and cooperation. Keeping your cool and staying present in the moment is key. Prioritize the issue, choosing your words deliberately if you aim for a meaningful conversation and long-term harmony.

Refrain from Underhanded Tactics

Personal attacks and manipulative tactics have no place in constructive communication. Such behavior only serves to create emotional distance. Ensure that your intent is to resolve the issue rather than "win" an argument.

Don't Shut Down

In emotionally charged situations, it's natural to retreat inward or "clam up." While it may offer a momentary escape, it leaves issues unresolved and could make your son feel ignored or undervalued. If you are inching toward emotional shutdown, the first step is to be transparent about your need for a break. Calmly tell your son that you're finding it hard to engage effectively and need a moment to collect your thoughts. Emphasize your commitment to resuming the dialogue, so it's clear you're not avoiding the issue.

Once you've taken your break—whether a walk around the block or a few minutes of deep breathing—return to the conversation as promised. Your consistency here is crucial; it sets a precedent for honest communication with your son. If you're concerned about the emotional charge coming back, take a break and go over the earlier advice on staying calm and focused. This will prepare you to reenter the conversation in a more constructive mindset.

Your credibility and the trust you're building with your son depend on following through. By doing so, you're resolving the matter at hand and modeling responsible emotional behavior.

Avoid Generalizations

General statements like "You never listen" or "You're always late" can create an emotional wall between you and your son when discussing concerns. These absolutes can worsen the situation, prompting defensiveness rather than encouraging resolution. Instead, aim to be specific. For example, say, "I noticed you were late coming home last night, and it worried me," instead of saying, "You're always late." Being clear and specific keeps the conversation constructive and opens the door for mutual understanding, focusing on resolving the matter rather than escalating tensions.

Active Listening

Active listening is a fundamental component of effective communication. Rather than merely hearing words, it involves a deep understanding of the underlying sentiments and intentions.

Full Attention

Dedicating full attention during a conversation signifies the value placed on the speaker's words. This focused approach ensures that the listener is comprehensively grasping the content and context of the discussion.

Engagement

Actively listening to a child reinforces their belief that their thoughts and feelings are important. This validation is essential for building self-esteem. For MY sons, it provides affirmation, and for CD sons, it confirms the weight of their words.

Active Listening Techniques

- **Use Nonverbal Responses:** Use nods and maintain eye contact. These gestures show engagement and understanding.

- **Ask for Clarification:** Pose questions such as, "Can you elaborate on that?" to ensure clarity.

- **Paraphrase:** Summarize what's been said to confirm understanding.

- **Avoid Interrupting:** Allow the speaker to complete their thoughts before responding. This respects their perspective and ensures comprehensive communication.

In summary, active listening is more than a communication tool; it's a means to strengthen the parent-son bond by ensuring clear understanding and mutual respect.

Use Neutral Language to Curb Defensiveness

The choice of words plays a crucial role in how your message is received. Accusatory language can shift the focus from resolving the issue to defending oneself, making constructive communication difficult. To avoid this, focus on the specific action or situation and share how it made you feel. There are two effective ways to do this: "We" statements and "I" statements.

Use "We" Statements

Using "we" statements suggests a team effort in problem-solving, encouraging a collaborative rather than adversarial discussion. This can ease tension and create an environment conducive to compromise.

Don't Say This
"You always leave the lights on, which raises the electricity bill."

Instead, Say This
"We have an increasing electricity bill, and leaving lights on adds to it. Could we work together to remember to turn them off?"

Using "we" transforms the dialogue into a joint venture for a solution instead of laying the blame, making it easier to engage in productive conversation.

Use "I" Statements

Using "I" statements allows you to express how a certain action affects you without sounding accusatory. This psychiatrist-endorsed method enables you to share your feelings and concerns in a nonconfrontational way.

Don't Say This
"You never listen to what I say; it feels like you don't care."

Instead, Say This
"I feel unheard when you don't seem to pay attention to what I'm saying. Listening is important to me in our relationship."

Focusing on your feelings and experiences prevents your son from becoming defensive, increasing the likelihood of a constructive dialogue. Both "we" and "I" statements foster open, honest, and less confrontational communication. They allow you to express your feelings and concerns in a manner that makes it easier for the other person to understand and empathize without feeling attacked or blamed.

Appreciate Silence with CDs

Engaging with a CD son often means navigating moments of quiet introspection. This introspective nature isn't indicative of detachment; it's the CD's way of deeply processing information and emotions. Recognizing and honoring these moments can lead to more authentic and meaningful interactions.

- Attend to his need for pauses in conversations. Allow him these moments to gather his thoughts, especially on deep or sensitive topics.

- Give him space in emotionally charged situations to step back and process. Avoid pressing a CD for immediate feedback or resolution to foster genuine communication.

- Create an environment where you view quiet moments not as emotional barriers but as opportunities for deeper understanding and connection.

Understanding and embracing these moments of silence lays the foundation for a relationship built on mutual respect and genuine connection. It sends a clear message: you value and recognize his unique way of processing the world around him.

Offer Regular Verbal Affirmations for MYs

For MY sons, words are not just utterances; they serve as affirming tokens of your love and approval. To resonate with their communication style, consider these strategies:

- Express your pride and admiration openly, especially after they achieve something, no matter how minor.

- Deliver compliments and praise. Consistent verbal reinforcement reinforces their sense of self-worth and encourages positive behavior.

- Acknowledge efforts and openness. A simple "I appreciate your hard work" or "I'm proud of you" can profoundly impact him.

Regularly offering verbal affirmations creates a supportive and validating environment in which MY sons appreciate and thrive.

Understand That Your Son May Communicate Differently than You

Our inherent nature, upbringing, life experiences, and personality types shape our communication styles. When seeking to understand your son, recognizing these nuances is vital. The way your son communicates is significantly influenced by his personality type, be it CD, MY, or Straddler.

CDs often value their inner sanctuary, retreating into themselves to process emotions or think profoundly. They communicate directly, emphasizing logic and brevity. Sometimes, their introspection can be misunderstood as distance or indifference. In contrast, MYs are expressive, conveying emotions passionately and openly. They might include stories, anecdotes, or embellishments in their communication, which can occasionally come off as overwhelming. Straddlers find a middle ground, displaying traits from both CDs and MYs. They're skilled at assessing situations and adjusting their communication style to match. Their balanced approach can be puzzling for those looking for a clear-cut response.

Factors to consider in understanding your son's communication include his response time, especially if he's a CD who may need more time for thought. His way of expressing emotions, as MYs are naturally expressive, while CDs might wait for the right moment to share feelings. And engagement in conversations, as Straddlers can move between deep, introspective discussions and animated chats. Cultivating patience and an open mind is essential. Every individual has a unique communication style, and by respecting these differences, you can build a stronger bond with your son, enabling genuine expression.

Lead by Example

The concept of leading by example is grounded in the understanding that actions often speak louder than words, especially in parent-child relationships. Children, including sons, whether they are CDs, MYs, or Straddlers, are keen observers. They absorb cues from their environment, with parents being primary role models.

- Maintain consistency between your spoken words and your actions. This alignment showcases your integrity and exemplifies the importance of honesty and reliability to your son.

- Practice and display healthy emotional management techniques. Use moments of emotional intensity as opportunities to teach, whether that's taking a deliberate pause when upset or employing positive self-talk in challenging situations.

- Ensure that your daily actions mirror the values you emphasize, such as kindness, respect, or perseverance. When your son observes these values in action, he's more likely to internalize them.

- Promote an atmosphere of open dialogue in your household. If you want your son to be open about his feelings, ensure he sees you doing the same, discussing both highs and lows.

- When mistakes happen, openly acknowledge them. By taking responsibility and implementing corrective actions, you emphasize the values of accountability, growth, and learning.

By embodying the traits and values you wish to instill in your son, you provide a tangible model for him to follow. This proactive approach not only strengthens the bond but also cultivates a foundation for your son's personal and social development.

Demonstrate Healthy Communication in and outside the Home

Communication is foundational to relationships. It's vital to show its effectiveness both inside and outside your home, as this significantly shapes your son's interpersonal abilities. To model healthy communication, foster an environment where open dialogue is encouraged and every voice matters. Whether it's about weekend plans or disagreements, make sure everyone feels they can express themselves. Active listening is equally important. When someone speaks, show your son the value of truly hearing them by maintaining eye contact, nodding to show understanding, and not interrupting. Communication isn't solely verbal. Body language, gestures, and facial expressions convey a lot. Demonstrate openness and attentiveness, especially when interacting with unique personalities, like CDs and MYs.

Disagreements are a natural part of human interactions, but the manner in which they're handled is crucial. It's beneficial to approach conflicts with calmness, focusing on solutions over blame, and emphasizing compromise and understanding. Empathy is a powerful tool in all communications. Show your son the importance of empathetic interactions, whether it's comforting someone or trying to understand another's viewpoint, like that of a CD or MY. Boundaries are also an essential component of effective communication. Highlight the significance of recognizing and respecting others' boundaries, be it a CD's preference for solitude or an MY's inclination for social interaction. It's crucial that the principles of healthy communication practiced at home are consistent in your external dealings, be it at community events, school functions, or everyday errands.

By exemplifying these communication tactics in diverse situations and with various personalities, you're equipping your son with skills beneficial for all aspects of his life. This approach reinforces the notion that every interaction offers a chance to understand, connect, and evolve.

Embrace Emotional Expression

Emotion serves as a profound connector in relationships. For young boys, understanding that expressing feelings isn't a weakness but strength is vital. This mindset promotes both intimacy and resilience. Parents play a crucial role in shaping this understanding, emphasizing that all emotions, from joy to sadness, are valid. Instead of classifying feelings, the focus should be on understanding and managing them.

Open dialogue is essential. Regular emotional check-ins and open-ended questions can help boys express their feelings. Parents should model vulnerability, showcasing that deep emotions can be shared with trust. For those struggling to articulate, creative outlets like art or music can be invaluable, especially for introspective individuals. When boys share their emotions, they should be met with understanding and empathy.

Avoiding stereotypes, like "Boys don't cry," and introducing diverse emotional role models can help challenge traditional views of masculinity. When emotions arise from challenges, it's an opportunity for collaborative problem-solving. By nurturing this emotional landscape, parents equip their sons for life, fostering resilience and genuine connections.

Show Your Son That You're Human Too

One of the most profound lessons you can impart to your children is the understanding of your shared humanity—that parents, too, have emotions, make mistakes, and continuously learn. Demonstrating your own humanity serves multiple purposes: it humanizes you in your son's eyes, makes him feel less isolated in his experiences, and teaches him to approach life with humility and empathy. Here's how you can authentically convey this lesson:

- **Share Personal Stories:** Recount instances from your past where you faced challenges, made mistakes, or overcame obstacles. This gives him insight into your life and shows him that struggles are a natural part of life.

- **Admit Mistakes:** If you realize you've made an error or handled a situation poorly, own up to it. Apologize genuinely and discuss how you could approach such situations differently.

- **Express Emotions Openly:** Let him see when you're sad, frustrated, or elated. Sharing emotions can foster closer bonds and show him it's okay to be in touch with one's feelings.

- **Seek His Opinion:** Occasionally, ask for his thoughts or advice on noncritical decisions or situations. It makes him feel valued and shows that you don't have all the answers and are open to learning.

- **Discuss Life's Uncertainties:** Speak about times when you felt uncertain or were navigating uncharted waters. It emphasizes that everyone faces times of doubt, regardless of age or experience.

- **Model Growth:** Show him you're still learning, whether picking up a new hobby, taking a course, or reading a book. Demonstrating a growth mindset reinforces the idea that learning is a lifelong journey.

- **Express Empathy:** When he shares his experiences, relate with similar emotions or situations you've faced, creating a bridge of understanding between you.

- **Handle Setbacks Gracefully:** If things don't go as planned, instead of getting overly frustrated, discuss it as a learning opportunity. Your approach to setbacks can shape his resilience and attitude toward challenges.

By letting your son see your vulnerabilities, strengths, mistakes, and growth, you're not just revealing your humanity but equipping him with tools for empathy, understanding, and resilience. He learns that to err is human, but the actual strength lies in recognizing those errors, learning from them, and growing.

Key Takeaways

Communication is the lifeline of every parent-child bond, bridging gaps and forging a deeper connection. In navigating the complex waters of your sons' ever-evolving emotional and mental landscapes, understanding and mastering the art of communication becomes paramount, irrespective of whether they lean toward the introspective realm of the CDs or the vocal sphere of the MYs.

- **Speak Without Conflict:** Express feelings and opinions, but navigate conversations to avoid confrontations. Approach matters thoughtfully to build understanding.

- **Delve Deeper in Listening:** Active listening involves immersing yourself in the conversation, understanding the underlying emotions, and respecting the sentiments conveyed.

- **Neutralize Your Tone:** Opt for "I feel" statements, which allow open dialogue without creating a defensive stance.

- **Respect the Quiet of CDs:** Understand that a CD son's silence is often a sign of introspection, not disinterest. Give space for reflection and eventual communication.

- **Celebrate the Vibrancy of MYs:** Regular affirmations resonate with MYs, assuring them that their feelings and expressions are valued and acknowledged.

- **Cherish Communication Differences:** Instead of molding your son's communication style to match yours, adapt and appreciate his unique way of connecting.

- **Demonstrate Constructive Conversations:** Your approach to communication sets a precedent. Showcase patience, understanding, and genuine connection, fostering a healthy communication model.

- **Look beyond Words:** Communication is holistic. Provide a comprehensive guide on how to nurture connections both verbally and nonverbally.

- **Promote Emotional Expression:** Encourage your son to openly discuss and process emotions, emphasizing the strength of vulnerability and emotional understanding.

- **Model Authenticity:** Display vulnerability and accept mistakes. By doing so, you reassure your son that imperfections are part of growth and learning.

Remember, communication with your son isn't about talking down or dictating. It's a dance—a balance of speaking and listening, understanding and expressing. By embracing these communication strategies, you're not just talking but building a legacy of trust, understanding, and deep connection. It's not merely about making noise but creating resonating harmonies in your relationship with your son.

Chapter Three

Building the Bond

The parent-child relationship is built on mutual trust, understanding, guidance, and affection. As children grow and develop, so too does the relationship parents share with them. The process of raising a son, whether he aligns more with the CD or MY personality type, comes with diverse experiences and challenges. Central to all these experiences is the fundamental desire for a meaningful connection.

In this chapter, we will explore specific methodologies suited to the distinctive characteristics of CDs and MYs. The goal is to strengthen the parent-son relationship, enabling it to adapt and thrive over time. Our focus is on appreciating your son's individuality while deepening trust, understanding, and love. By examining different approaches, we aim to provide parents with tools to convey consistent love and support, ensuring sons feel recognized and appreciated. This exploration goes beyond mere parenting tactics; it's about cultivating a relationship rooted in mutual respect, balancing both unity and individuality.

Talk to Your Son

Conversations play a pivotal role in fostering understanding and connection, especially with your sons. In today's digital age, where screen time often overshadows face-to-face interaction, carving out moments for genuine dialogue becomes increasingly significant. Regular conversations with your son lay a foundation for trust, assuring him he can approach you with any issue, big or small. Through these discussions, you gain insight into his world, encompassing his friends, passions, obstacles, and aspirations, enabling you to offer pertinent advice and backing.

Conversations also serve as a platform to express your affection and concern, reaffirming your commitment to his well-being and happiness. While it's an avenue for you to share wisdom, life lessons, and personal experiences, it's equally important to be receptive, understanding that your sons often bring fresh, enlightening perspectives to the table. This open channel of communication also simplifies broaching more complex topics, be it peer pressure, relationships, or other potential challenges in his life. By actively listening to him, you bolster his self-esteem, reinforcing that his feelings, ideas, and viewpoints are valued.

Life's hectic pace notwithstanding, these connecting moments should always be a priority. Whether it's a casual chat during a car ride, a discussion over dinner, or a heart-to-heart just before bedtime, it's essential to seize these moments. Doing so assures him that, irrespective of his age or the subject at hand, you remain a constant source of support, always ready to listen, empathize, and engage.

Take the Lead in Further Developing the Bond

Building and nurturing the bond with your sons often requires a proactive approach. While you might wish for your sons to approach you, the onus of forging and preserving this relationship often rests on the parent, given that you are their primary guides to the world. Being proactive in this relationship is foundational for several reasons.

First, it sets a precedent. When parents actively engage and invest in the relationship, it teaches sons that meaningful relationships require effort and active involvement. By initiating conversations, especially on challenging topics or sharing personal sentiments, you signal to your son the presence of a safe and open environment. This gesture invites transparency and trust.

As children grow, their needs and ways of communicating undergo changes. By taking the initiative, parents can stay in tune with these shifts, ensuring they adjust and adapt, making the bond both relevant and resilient as time progresses. Being ahead of the curve also enables parents to address potential challenges or misunderstandings promptly, promoting a culture where issues are confronted directly and resolved transparently.

Every proactive effort made by parents, be it a gesture of support, understanding, or connection, underlines the concept of unconditional love. It sends a message that regardless of situations, the love and bond shared remain unwavering. However, while shaping this relationship, it's crucial to ensure mutual respect. While guiding and offering direction, it's equally vital to respect your son's individuality and autonomy. This balance showcases that relationships are based on mutual regard and thoughtfulness.

The relationship between a parent and a child is dynamic and continually changing. By actively steering this bond, parents guarantee that it not only persists but also evolves into a deep-rooted source of support, solace, and direction for both parties.

Show Your CD You Respect His Mind

CDs, inherently introspective, inhabit a realm bursting with rich thoughts, ideas, and insights. To nurture a bond with your CD son, recognizing and valuing this depth is essential. Engage actively and attentively whenever he unveils his reflections, understanding that a CD's articulations often emerge from profound contemplation. Dive deep into subjects he's fervent about, for instance, a cherished book, hobby, or an academic venture, as this genuine interest communicates profound respect for his choices.

Acknowledging his need for introspection is vital. Create an environment where he can comfortably immerse in quietude, be it for reading or simply to traverse his thoughts. In discussions or decisions, seeking his input not only leverages his analytical prowess but also underlines the significance you place on his perspective. Exercising patience, especially when he's engrossed in thought or a task, underscores respect for his concentrated focus. When he achieves, whether academically or through a unique insight, it's important to celebrate not just the achievement itself but the intricate thought mechanism driving it. And when he takes moments to process information or respond, grant him the requisite time, with no pressure.

Through these gestures of understanding and appreciation, you fortify a relationship anchored in mutual respect and trust, emphatically conveying that you not only love him but deeply esteem his cerebral approach to the world.

Show Your MY You Respect His Expression

MYs radiate a natural expressiveness, translating their feelings, reflections, and inspirations into outward expressions. This innate vivacity and spontaneity form an integral facet of their persona. Deepening your relationship with your MY son hinges on fully embracing and valuing this vibrant demeanor.

When he narrates experiences or expounds on topics with fervor, immerse yourself in his stories. Your questions, enthusiasm, and encouragement amplify his narrative zeal. Champion his passions wholeheartedly. If he's drawn to the arts, music, or theater, stand as his most ardent supporter—attend his showcases, revel in his artistic endeavors, and share his exuberance.

It's essential to equip him with avenues for expression. This could manifest as enrolling him in a specialized class, furnishing him with creative tools, or simply offering an attentive ear whenever he's eager to converse. MYs often display their emotions openly, so be present to rejoice in their moments of elation and offer solace during downturns. Cultivating an atmosphere of open communication, devoid of judgment, ensures he feels both valued and comprehended. Acknowledge his intrinsic need for interaction, be it casual conversations, spending time with friends, or team participation. And rather than attempting to temper his animated spirit, communicate your appreciation for his expressive essence.

In valuing and acknowledging your MY son's unique communicative style, you not only fortify your bond but also empower him with confidence, reinforcing that his mode of interaction is both respected and treasured.

Have Meaningful Interactions with Your Son

Interacting deeply and intentionally with your son goes beyond the boundaries of casual conversations and routine activities. These profound engagements cultivate trust, deepen understanding, and solidify the bond shared between parent and child.

To enrich these moments, it's beneficial to allocate designated times free from external interruptions, ensuring the focus is solely on the two of you. This can manifest as regular dinner dates or periodic outings. Engaging in activities that mutually resonate, be it gardening, attending a workshop, or watching films, helps in strengthening shared interests. To encourage a deeper exploration of thoughts and feelings, posing open-ended questions can be more effective than those eliciting simple affirmative or negative responses.

Active listening is paramount. When your son articulates his thoughts, being mentally present, comprehending his sentiments, and responding with consideration ensures he feels genuinely acknowledged. It's equally beneficial to open up about your personal experiences, challenges, and insights, paving the way for him to reciprocate with his narratives. By actively seeking his opinions on various matters, from household decisions to book recommendations, you impart a sense of value and importance to his perspectives.

Introducing special traditions, such as a distinctive greeting, an annual journey, or a communal journal, creates lasting memories unique to your relationship. Above all, authenticity remains the cornerstone of these interactions. Genuine emotions, responses, and feedback foster a trusting environment.

By investing in moments marked by intentionality and genuineness, not only do you familiarize yourself more deeply with your son, but you also convey his significance in your life. These enriched connections evolve into treasured recollections, establishing a bedrock of mutual respect, understanding, and affection that spans a lifetime.

Engage in Activities Your CD or MY Enjoy

Understanding the individual predilections of CD and MY personalities in terms of relaxation and bonding endeavors is vital. It can pave the way for a deeper and more meaningful connection with your son. Here's how you can effectively engage with a CD personality:

For the CD Son

CD sons often find solace in activities that allow them to immerse in deep thought or concentrate on intricate details. Reading together offers such an opportunity. Delving into a book series concurrently and then allocating moments to discuss feelings and interpretations about the narrative can be immensely rewarding. Similarly, the act of puzzle building provides a platform for both concentration and teamwork. Engaging in detailed arts and crafts, like model building, sketching, or even woodworking, can resonate with their meticulous nature.

Nature-themed endeavors can also appeal to CD personalities. Star gazing, for instance, isn't merely about identifying constellations; the tranquility of the activity often fosters profound conversations. Equipping yourselves with a bird guide and binoculars for bird-watching can transform an outing into an observational adventure. Taking a relaxed walk, cameras in tow, to capture nature can also be a way to see the world through his lens, allowing you to appreciate his perspective.

Fostering a CD son's innate curiosity and analytical inclination can be achieved through focused learning experiences. Workshops, particularly in areas like coding, present an environment for him to dive deep and refine his capabilities. Museums and exhibits, especially those with a historical or scientific bent, cater to his analytical side, offering insights and knowledge.

The comforts of home can also be a backdrop for bonding. Cooking together, where you both select a recipe and craft it in unison, can be both a calming and gratifying experience. Opting for movie nights, especially with films renowned for their complex storylines or introspective themes, can be a wonderful way to wind down while still engaging his thoughtful nature. Through these varied activities, you acknowledge and value the unique disposition of your CD son, fortifying the bond you share.

For the MY Son

For the MY son, consider incorporating activities that cater to his energetic and interactive nature. Engaging in team sports such as soccer or basketball or spending a day exploring the thrills of an adventure park can be highly enjoyable. Expressive outlets like dance classes offer a wonderful platform for his vibrant energy. Opt for learning environments that promote group interaction; drama classes, group art projects, or interactive displays at science centers can be particularly appealing.

Socially, consider hosting game nights with board or video games that involve multiple players or attending community fairs and local concerts that align with his extroverted tendencies. To stimulate expressive conversations, you might organize debate nights on interesting topics or share personal stories, encouraging him to reciprocate. By aligning activities with your son's personality, you not only make him feel understood and appreciated but also enrich the bond through shared experiences, fostering deeper connections and mutual respect.

Create an Environment That Allows for Open Communication

Cultivating an environment that fosters open communication is crucial in building a strong bond of trust and understanding with your son, regardless of whether he identifies as a CD, MY, or Straddler. To achieve this, it's vital to ensure that he feels his voice is both heard and valued.

One of the primary ways to nurture this bond is through nonjudgmental listening. This means approaching your son's experiences and feelings with an open mind, free from immediate judgments, allowing him to feel that his thoughts are valid and won't be met with criticism. Depending on your son's personality, designate specific environments conducive to conversation. For CDs, a quiet, distraction-free space might be more effective, whereas MYs might benefit from dynamic settings like walking or doing an activity.

It's beneficial to set aside dedicated times for routine check-ins, where you both can share updates about your week, the highs, lows, and everything in between. If your son leans more toward the CD spectrum, consider encouraging him to journal, as this can often help articulate feelings before verbalizing them.

When giving or receiving feedback, ensure it is constructive, focusing on solutions rather than problems. Using "I" statements can help frame discussions that are less confrontational and more about expressing feelings. For instance, instead of saying, "You always do this," you can express, "I feel upset when this happens." This encourages a more open and understanding dialogue.

To enhance the quality of conversations, consider designating tech-free times or zones within your home where electronic distractions are minimized. If there are topics your son isn't comfortable discussing, respect his boundaries and allow him the space he needs. Engage actively when he opens up, showing empathy and avoiding multitasking. Encouraging open-ended questions can also stimulate richer conversations. Instead of asking, "Did you have a good day?" you might prompt with, "What was the highlight of your day?"

Laying the groundwork for open communication strengthens the relationship, enabling both of you to navigate challenges collaboratively. It's not merely about avoiding conflicts but about building resilience to face them together and learning to navigate the complexities of life as a unified team.

Let Your CD or MY Son Tell You What He Needs

In the journey of parenthood, understanding your child's unique needs and desires becomes pivotal. This connection becomes more profound when you consider the distinct nuances presented by the personality types of CD and MY. Here, you delve into the tailored ways of navigating these waters to create a bond where your son feels understood and valued.

For Your CD Son

- Comfortable environments are conducive to communication: CDs thrive in tranquil settings where their thoughts can flow uninhibited.

- A listening ear is crucial: Patience is key as CDs process emotions internally and may take time before expressing them.

- Open-ended queries are beneficial: Questions that aren't limited to "yes" or "no" answers can lead to richer conversations.

- Affirmation and appreciation are essential: Expressing gratitude when your CD son shares his feelings fosters mutual respect.

For Your MY Son

- Active engagement is appreciated: MYs derive validation from interactive conversations.

- Physical touch holds significance: Reassuring touches or hugs can convey feelings of understanding and affection for an MY.

- In-depth exploration is beneficial: Beyond the words of an MY, the underlying emotions are important for a comprehensive understanding.

- Regular check-ins are encouraged: Offering avenues for open dialogue ensures he feels comfortable expressing himself.

- Passions should be celebrated: Being supportive of his interests or hobbies strengthens the bond and reinforces his sense of value.

In parent-child relationships, as in other interpersonal dynamics, understanding and respecting individual needs is essential for a positive bond. Using these strategies and actively engaging with your son can strengthen trust and mutual respect. It's through these detailed interactions that significant connections are made. By dedicating time and effort, you're fostering a lasting bond, ensuring your son feels acknowledged and valued. Approach this relationship with attentiveness and dedication, and observe as your interactions with your son develop into a series of shared experiences and mutual respect.

Praise Him—Don't Only Point Out Faults

Affirming your son, whether he leans toward the introspective nature of a CD or the vibrancy of an MY, helps to nurture your bond. Children naturally seek validation from their primary caregivers, and consistent recognition of your son's efforts, strengths, and individuality can substantially bolster his self-esteem. Conversely, perpetual criticism without acknowledgment of his achievements can erode his self-confidence.

Every milestone, whether it's mastering a new skill or showing empathy, deserves celebration. Such positive reinforcements motivate him to keep pushing his boundaries. However, when guidance is required, the manner in which it's delivered matters. Instead of pinpointing errors directly, steer him toward finding solutions, fostering an environment of growth and learning.

Strive to create a balanced atmosphere where praise notably outweighs critiques. It's essential to recognize and celebrate the journey as much as the destination, teaching him that effort is just as commendable as the outcome. For a CD, a thoughtful note or a deep conversation can serve as a meaningful acknowledgment, while an MY might appreciate more public praise.

Remember, your positive affirmations shape how your son views himself and the world. Such consistent validation equips him with a resilient sense of self-worth that he carries into adulthood. By cultivating an environment where he feels perpetually acknowledged and valued, you fortify your bond and empower him with the self-belief to navigate life's complexities. This balance between encouragement and constructive feedback anchors the relationship, laying a foundation of mutual respect and trust.

Tell Your Son You Love Him

Saying "I love you" to your son is not just a sentimental gesture; it serves a pivotal role in his emotional development. While children with unique personality traits may perceive or internalize this expression differently, the essential takeaway for both types signifies emotional assurance and a feeling of belonging.

For the CD Son

CDs are introspective by nature. They spend considerable time in internal reflection, often pondering over emotional nuances and the dynamics of their relationships. For a CD son, the deliberate verbal affirmation of love can function as a touchstone of emotional security. While the verbal affirmation is potent, its impact can be amplified when coupled with other forms of emotional expression that CDs may find meaningful.

For instance, you might pen down your feelings in the form of handwritten letters, which provide them with a tangible form of your emotional investment that they can return to when needed. Another approach is to engage in one-on-one conversations that delve into emotional and philosophical discussions. By doing this, you validate not only their emotional needs but also their intellectual depth, amplifying the impact of your affirmation.

For the MY Son

MYs are more extroverted, relishing spontaneous expressions of emotion and deriving energy from social interactions. For MY sons, immediate and physical affirmations often resonate powerfully. These can take the form of spontaneous hugs, high-fives, or an encouraging pat on the back.

Because MYs live in the moment, timing your affirmation to coincide with instances when they are visibly joyful or have achieved something allows you to validate not only their achievements but their emotional states as well. This spontaneous but thoughtful affirmation reinforces your emotional support, creating a robust emotional environment.

Cultural and Familial Factors

Many families, owing to cultural or generational norms, might not commonly express love verbally. If this has been your experience, attempting to articulate your love can signify a pivotal shift in family dynamics, benefiting your child's emotional health.

If your culture traditionally refrains from overt emotional expression, you may need to consider incremental approaches. Initially, you could opt for actions that are emotionally equivalent to saying "I love you," such as spending quality time with your son or offering acts of service. As comfort levels increase, progressing to verbal affirmations can be a natural next step.

For those who grew up in environments where parents seldom or never verbalized their love, taking the step to do so with your own children can feel daunting. Here, individual or family counseling can provide a supportive framework for understanding the emotional inhibitions you might grapple with and offer strategies for overcoming them.

The consistent articulation of love gains heightened importance during challenging phases, such as periods of personal struggle or the turbulent years of adolescence. A steady flow of emotional affirmation serves as a stabilizing element, equipping your son with the emotional fortitude to navigate complex situations.

While the spoken word is powerful, reinforcing verbal expressions of love through consistent actions magnifies their impact. Engaging in quality time, extending emotional or practical support during challenges, and taking the time to celebrate achievements are all ways to express love.

In sum, the act of consistently telling your son "I love you" contributes significantly to his emotional well-being, offering him a foundational sense of security and validation. This remains true across different personality types, each of which may require slight adjustments in your approach. Overcoming cultural and familial barriers to expressing this sentiment can be transformative for both you and your child, setting a new emotional standard for future generations.

Key Takeaways

Building a bond with your son is a lifelong journey that begins from his earliest days and continues to develop as he grows. The key to fortifying this relationship lies not just in the grand gestures but also in the everyday interactions. Regardless of whether your son leans toward the contemplative tendencies of a CD or the vibrant energy of an MY, the foundation of the bond remains the same: genuine connection, respect, and love.

- **Start Conversations:** Engage your son in both deep and casual dialogues. Use every chat to reinforce your bond, ensuring he feels heard.

- **Lead the Bonding:** Don't just wait; actively seek opportunities to nurture and deepen the relationship.

- **Appreciate CD Depth:** Engage in introspective discussions, tapping into your CD son's cerebral nature.

- **Celebrate MY Vibrancy:** Dive into lively exchanges, embracing your MY son's enthusiastic way of connecting.

- **Value Moments Together:** Focus on the quality of interactions, ensuring that every shared moment counts.

- **Engage in His Activities:** Immerse yourself in what your son loves, be it introspective tasks for CDs or energetic ones for MYs.

- **Foster Open Dialogue:** Create an environment that encourages open communication, where all thoughts and feelings are expressed freely.

- **Listen Actively:** When your son speaks up about his needs or wishes, be receptive and show that his input matters.

- **Provide Balanced Feedback:** Offer guidance, but always mix constructive feedback with praise. Highlight his achievements and strengths.

- **Affirm Your Love Regularly:** Speak affirmations and remind your son of your love and trust frequently.

Consider that the relationship with your son is comparable to a developing organism. With consistent care, understanding, and mutual respect, it will mature and strengthen. Regardless of whether he identifies as a CD or an MY, the fundamental need remains consistent: your son seeks connection, validation, and affirmation. Applying these insights can foster a relationship that endures through various challenges.

Chapter Four

Effective Socialization

Navigating the complexities of social interactions and relationships is a dynamic process. Every child, whether a CD or an MY, engages in this process with individual tendencies and external influences. As caregivers, your responsibility extends beyond mere observation; you are active participants, aiding and reinforcing while recognizing their distinct social patterns. This chapter outlines various approaches aligned with these distinct social predispositions. With specific strategies and purposeful interactions, the goal is to establish an environment where every son confidently engages in his social realm. The focus will be on encouraging genuine interactions, implementing thoughtful boundaries, and enabling your sons to develop relationships congruent with their individuality and worldview.

Understand CDs' Need for Solitude and MYs' Social Inclinations

To foster genuine connections for your sons and prepare them for a world teeming with diverse personalities, it's crucial to recognize their innate social tendencies.

CDs often find solace in their inner world. Solitude isn't a sign of loneliness for them but a chosen sanctuary where they recharge and reflect. These quiet moments allow them to process emotions, thoughts, and daily experiences at their own pace. It's essential not to misconstrue their need for alone time as reclusiveness or aloofness. Instead, appreciate it as their way of maintaining emotional equilibrium.

For MYs, socializing is like oxygen. Their spirit thrives on interactions, whether playful banter, group activities, or spontaneous plans. Their energy is contagious, drawing others into their orbit. They recharge amidst company, finding solitude occasionally stifling. Recognizing their inherent need to be amidst people and respecting it is crucial for their emotional well-being.

Understanding these contrasting social needs is pivotal. While it might be tempting to push a CD to be more outgoing or ask an MY to "tone it down," it's imperative to approach their inclinations respectfully. The key is to offer opportunities that align with their natural tendencies, ensuring they feel understood and supported.

Encourage Activities Catering to Both Personalities

When encouraging activities that cater to both the introspective CDs and the exuberant MYs, the goal is to find a balance. Activities should respect and amplify the unique strengths of each personality type, ensuring neither feels overwhelmed nor sidelined.

For CDs, it's vital to provide environments where they can delve deep into introspection without feeling pressured to interact constantly. Their comfort often lies in spaces where they can observe, reflect, and process at their own pace. MYs thrive in dynamic and interactive settings. They flourish in environments where they can express themselves, engage in conversations, and actively take part.

To cater to both personalities, choose activities that have elements of both individual focus and collective interaction. This duality ensures that CDs have moments of solitude and introspection, while MYs get their fill of vibrant interactions.

It's essential to ensure that both personality types feel valued in these shared activities. Providing opportunities for mutual appreciation will foster a sense of inclusivity. As caregivers, being observant and adaptive to their responses can aid in fine-tuning these shared experiences, creating a more harmonious balance between solitude and socialization.

Plan Activities That Meet Your CDs' or MYs' Social Needs

To truly nurture your son's social development, it's essential to plan activities tailored to their unique personality needs. Recognizing and honoring these differences will foster a healthy sense of self-worth and belonging. Here are targeted activities catering to the specific social needs of CDs and MYs:

For Your CD Son

- Solo Projects: Building model kits, painting, or individual musical instrument practice. These activities allow your CD to be engrossed in a task, offering introspective moments and a sense of achievement.

- Nature Retreats: Solo hikes, bird-watching, or fishing. The quiet, natural environment offers the tranquility CDs often crave, helping them connect deeply with their surroundings.

- Journaling or Writing: Maintaining a daily journal, writing short stories or poetry. This allows CDs to articulate and process their thoughts and emotions privately.

- Skill-Based Classes: Pottery classes, coding lessons, or photography workshops. While these might be group settings, the focus on individual tasks allows CDs to work at their own pace and interact as they see fit.

- Book Clubs with Small Groups: Small group meetings allow CDs to have deep, meaningful discussions in a comfortable setting without feeling overwhelmed by large crowds.

For Your MY Son

- Group Sports: Soccer, basketball, or relay races. MYs thrive in team dynamics, enjoying both the game and the camaraderie it brings.

- Group Workshops: Drama classes, group painting sessions, or cooking classes. These foster interaction and collaboration and allow MYs to share experiences and learn from peers.

- Social Gatherings: Organizing or attending parties, picnics, or group trips. These settings satiate the MY's inherent need for broader social interactions.

- Community Service: Volunteering at local shelters, taking part in community clean-up drives, or organizing charity events. MYs often find fulfillment in activities that involve interaction and serve a larger purpose.

- Interactive Games and Activities: Board games, video games with online communities, or escape rooms. These activities offer the thrill of social engagement and shared achievement that MYs often seek.

Remember to gauge and respect your son's comfort levels when planning these activities. Forcing a CD into large social gatherings or pushing an MY into prolonged solitude can lead to stress and resentment. It's a delicate balance—understanding their intrinsic needs and offering activities that help them thrive, grow, and feel valued.

Appreciate MY's Need for Broader Social Engagements

The vivacious spirit of a MY son isn't just about the energy he exudes. It's also about his innate desire to connect with a larger circle, engage, and experience the world with others by his side. While every child deserves to have their social inclinations understood and nurtured, an MY's need for broader social engagements is particularly pronounced.

- **Value of Broadened Horizons:** MYs gain a wealth of knowledge and experiences from diverse interactions. Engaging with a variety of individuals helps shape their perspective, instilling a sense of openness and acceptance toward different viewpoints and cultures.

- **Energetic Release:** These broader engagements allow MYs to channel their abundant energy constructively. Whether joining a local sports team, taking part in dance troupes, or attending vibrant gatherings, they crave activities that resonate with their energetic demeanor.

- **Building Social Skills:** Being part of larger groups helps MYs develop crucial life skills like teamwork, leadership, and effective communication. It instills the ability to navigate complex social scenarios with grace and understanding.

- **Emotional Health:** Broader engagements offer MYs an outlet for their emotions. Expressing joy, sharing concerns, or merely being in the company of peers can have a therapeutic effect, promoting positive mental health.

- **Feedback and Growth:** Engaging in larger groups allows MYs to receive feedback, both positive and constructive, from a diverse set of individuals. This can be a powerful tool for personal growth and self-awareness.

As a caregiver, it's essential to:

- **Facilitate Opportunities:** Whether enrolling them in community clubs, supporting attendance at local events, or merely setting up playdates with a broad group of peers, creating opportunities for diverse engagements is crucial.

- **Engage with Them:** Occasionally join in these social activities. It provides a dual advantage: understanding your son's social dynamics and reinforcing your bond by sharing experiences.

- **Set Boundaries:** While promoting social engagements, it's equally important to set boundaries. Ensure your MY son understands the importance of balance and safety in diverse social scenarios.

- **Open Conversations:** Regularly discuss his experiences, feelings, and learnings from these engagements. It helps in gauging comfort levels and addressing any concerns he might have.

Your MY son's need for broader social engagements isn't just a whim or phase. It's a core aspect of his personality. By appreciating, understanding, and nurturing this intrinsic need, you provide him a platform to thrive socially, emotionally, and mentally.

Set Age-Appropriate Boundaries for Your Son

Boundaries play a pivotal role in a child's development, guiding them toward responsible and respectful behaviors while ensuring their safety and well-being. For both CDs and MYs, age-appropriate boundaries are essential, albeit their specific needs might differ. Setting clear and consistent limits fosters an environment of trust, respect, and mutual understanding, allowing your son to navigate the world confidently and responsibly.

The Importance of Boundaries

One primary purpose of boundaries is to ensure safety. As your son ventures out, be it in the digital realm or the physical world, these set limits act as a protective shield, safeguarding him from potential harm. These boundaries inculcate a sense of respect—not only for oneself but also for others. By understanding where one's limits lie, the child learns the significance of personal space, the essence of consent, and the overarching importance of mutual respect.

Boundaries instill a sense of accountability and responsibility. They teach your son that actions have repercussions. When rules are established, it becomes clear that veering off the path has consequences. This realization fosters a mature understanding of responsibility, ensuring he becomes accountable for his actions and decisions. Boundaries don't just set limits; they lay the foundation for trust, understanding, and a responsible transition into adulthood.

Tailoring Boundaries for CDs

CDs often require solitude to recharge and process their thoughts. To accommodate this, it's essential to set boundaries concerning their personal space. This can mean understanding the significance of a closed door or respecting their periods of quiet reflection. On the emotional front, CDs may not always share their feelings readily. While it's beneficial to foster an environment that encourages open communication, it's equally crucial not to pressure them to share beyond what they're comfortable with.

Tailoring Boundaries for MYs

MYs are naturally drawn to social engagements. As they navigate through social scenarios, especially during their teenage years, it's important to establish clear rules about their social interactions. This includes guidelines on how frequently they can engage in social outings, curfews, and understanding the company they keep. Given their expressive nature, MYs wear their emotions on their sleeves. While their openness is a strength, it's also necessary to guide them on appropriate manners and times to express their emotions, ensuring they convey their feelings respectfully and constructively.

Effective Implementation

- **Consistency:** For boundaries to be effective, they must be consistent. Changing rules frequently can confuse and frustrate your son.

- **Clear Communication:** Ensure that your son understands the reasons behind each boundary. Open dialogue can prevent misunderstandings and resistance.

- **Involve Him in the Process:** Especially as he grows older, involve him in setting some of his boundaries. It instills a sense of responsibility and makes him more inclined to adhere to them.

- **Re-evaluation:** As your son matures, revisit and adjust the boundaries. What's appropriate for a five-year-old is probably not suitable for a fifteen-year-old.

Enforcing Boundaries

Setting boundaries is an integral aspect of guiding your son's development. When boundaries are crossed, it's essential to allow him to understand the natural consequences, provided they are safe. This firsthand experience often serves as a potent learning tool. While enforcing these guidelines, maintaining a composed demeanor is crucial. By calmly explaining the reasons for such boundaries and their significance, it makes the purpose clear. Further, when he adheres to these boundaries, it's beneficial to use positive reinforcement. Recognizing and appreciating his compliance can further cement the desired behavior.

However, it's imperative to understand that these boundaries aren't merely restrictions. Their primary aim is to aid your son in his journey to become a well-rounded, considerate, and accountable individual. By discerning his specific needs and instituting age and personality-appropriate boundaries, you're providing him with the framework to confidently traverse life's complexities.

Encourage Your Son to Spend Time with Friends

Friendships play a monumental role in an individual's life, particularly during the formative years. These bonds offer emotional support, create a sense of belonging, and present opportunities for personal growth and social development. Whether your son identifies as a CD or a MY, fostering strong, healthy friendships is crucial. However, how each personality type interacts with friends might vary, requiring a nuanced approach to encouragement.

The Value of Friendships

Friendships play a pivotal role in a child's growth and development. They serve as vital emotional pillars, offering support when needed. Friends act as confidants, providing a listening ear and understanding challenges that your son may face in a manner that adults sometimes might not grasp. Beyond emotional support, these relationships also contribute significantly to skill development. Through regular interactions with peers, your son can hone essential life skills, such as communication, empathy, and problem-solving. By befriending individuals from various backgrounds, he is exposed to a tapestry of experiences and worldviews. This exposure can help to broaden his perspectives, nurture values of tolerance, and cultivate an open-minded approach to the world around him.

Encouraging CDs to Socialize

CDs often feel most at ease in smaller, more intimate social settings. Encouraging your CD son to engage in activities with a few close friends can be beneficial. This could range from hosting a movie night focused on thought-provoking films to arranging evenings where board games that require strategic thinking are played. These activities align well with a CD's tendency to favor meaningful, depth-oriented interactions.

Structured Social Activities

CDs might also enjoy structured social activities that allow for intellectual or emotional engagement. Consider suggesting they join clubs or gatherings where deep discussions are the norm—book clubs or philosophy circles, for instance. Activities like nature walks, which provide a serene setting conducive to deep conversations, can also serve as excellent social avenues for CDs.

Respect for Solitude

While socialization is important, it's crucial to acknowledge a CD's intrinsic need for solitude. Overstimulation from too much social interaction can be draining for them. As a parent, respecting their boundaries and giving them the space for alone time is imperative. Strike a balance between encouraging social activities and allowing periods of solitude for self-reflection and recharge.

Encouraging MYs to Engage

MYs usually thrive on the dynamism and energy of group settings. Given their extroverted nature, they are often eager to engage in activities that involve larger groups. This could range from participating in sports teams to becoming members of clubs that align with their interests—be it music, drama, or community service.

Broadening Social Horizons

It's also advantageous for your MY son to socialize with individuals from diverse social, cultural, and interest groups. Encourage him to step out of his comfort zone and befriend people who can offer different perspectives and experiences. This broadens his social skill set and expands his worldview.

Open and Inviting Home Environment

Creating an environment at home that is conducive to social interaction can be beneficial for MYs. Ensure your home feels welcoming to your son's friends, perhaps by setting up dedicated spaces where they can gather or offering to host events that he and his friends would enjoy. By doing this, you also gain an insightful glimpse into his evolving social circle, which is invaluable for tracking his social development.

By understanding the distinct social needs and preferences of your son, be he a CD or MY, you can offer targeted support that aligns with his personality type. This approach enhances not only his social skills but also contributes to a more nuanced emotional development.

Nurturing Positive Friendships

Engaging in open dialogue with your son about his friendships is a cornerstone of ensuring he aligns himself with positive influences. This involves regular discussions about the intrinsic qualities that define a good friend and emphasizing the paramount importance of mutual respect in any relationship. However, alongside encouraging robust friendships, it's equally vital to establish and communicate clear boundaries. These can pertain to time spent at friends' homes, adhering to curfews, and understanding other related familial expectations. To stay subtly connected to his developing social world, consider offering to facilitate their group activities. Simple gestures, such as driving your son and his friends to movies or parks, can provide insights without appearing overly intrusive.

Building Resilience

Every friendship experiences its difficulties. It's crucial to teach your son the importance of conflict resolution skills. By doing so, he'll learn to navigate these rough patches gracefully, emphasizing open communication and a deep-seated understanding of different perspectives. As he grows and interacts more with his peers, he's likely to encounter various forms of peer pressure. To fortify him against such influences, equip him with the tools and guidance, ensuring he adheres to his core values and consistently makes well-informed decisions that reflect his true self.

By promoting the value of friendships and understanding the unique social needs of CDs and MYs, you can guide your son toward forming and maintaining meaningful, lasting bonds. These relationships enhance his current life experience and set the foundation for healthy interpersonal dynamics in adulthood.

Socialize as a Family

Engaging in collective activities as a family unit holds immense significance in the life of every child, whether he identifies as a CD or an MY. The bonds forged during these shared experiences lay the groundwork for deeper connections, establishing a sense of security, identity, and shared values.

Family time is a tapestry woven with traditions, shared experiences, and the creation of memories that will be cherished for years. It offers a safe space where your son can freely express himself, knowing he's surrounded by the unconditional love and acceptance of his family. These shared moments solidify the bonds between family members, fostering understanding and mutual respect.

Creating an environment where everyone's preferences are acknowledged and valued is essential. While CDs might lean toward quieter family activities, such as board games or movie nights at home, MYs might find joy in more energetic outings like picnics or family trips. Integrating a mix of both types of activities ensures that everyone's needs are met, fostering a sense of inclusion.

Family activities offer a unique opportunity for open conversations. Whether discussing the day's events, reflecting on shared experiences, or planning future adventures, these dialogues enable family members to voice their thoughts, concerns, and aspirations. It encourages your son to share, knowing his voice holds weight and importance within the family setting.

In our modern age, bustling with commitments and distractions, carving out dedicated family time is paramount. It's not just about the duration but the quality of the time spent together. Ensure that electronic devices and external distractions are minimal, allowing for authentic interactions.

Family socialization not only strengthens the bond within the immediate family but also offers a model for your son's future interactions. He learns the values of trust, understanding, compromise, and the importance of quality time. This foundation will undoubtedly influence his future relationships, emphasizing mutual respect and understanding.

Promoting family time is an investment. It's about prioritizing moments of shared joy, laughter, understanding, and connection, ensuring that your son grows up in an environment rich in love, mutual respect, and a strong sense of belonging.

Foster Independence

The journey from boyhood to adulthood is underscored by the gradual shift toward autonomy. While the protective instinct of parents remains ever-present, fostering independence in your son is essential for his growth. Whether your son resonates more with the CD or MY personality, independence is a keystone in their path to self-realization and maturity.

The Value of Independence

The value of fostering independence in your son cannot be overstated. When he's taught to navigate situations independently, he not only cultivates resilience and adaptability but also becomes adept at handling life's varied challenges. Empowering him to take charge of his choices also equips him with the invaluable skill of decision-making, making him understand that each choice comes with its own set of consequences. This sense of independence paves the way for self-discovery, instilling confidence. Through this journey, he grows into a self-reliant man, ready to face the world.

Guiding CDs toward Independence

Encouraging CDs to embark on solo projects or hobbies can help to nurture their introspective nature. These activities allow them to connect with their passions, fostering a sense of accomplishment and self-awareness. Considering their inherent value for solitude, it's beneficial to designate a personal sanctuary within the home. This space serves as a haven where they can retreat, engage in reading, or partake in any solitary pursuit that brings them joy and introspection. As they navigate through life, it's crucial to nudge them toward scenarios that might be slightly outside their comfort zone. Such exposures, whether taking on grocery shopping or venturing out to a workshop alone, not only build their confidence but also equip them with diverse experiences that aid their personal growth.

Guiding MYs toward Independence

MYs inherently flourish in social environments, so guiding them toward independence can be achieved by tapping into this trait. Encouraging them to take the lead in group activities or projects can be a wonderful way to teach responsibility while catering to their extroverted tendencies. As they grow, allowing them the freedom to attend events, workshops, or classes that resonate with their passions can be pivotal. Such experiences enhance their skill set and offer them opportunities to build their network and foster independent interactions. Motivating them to take charge of community projects or spearhead school activities can be vital in nurturing their leadership skills. By championing such initiatives, they contribute positively to their surroundings and learn the value of responsibility, teamwork, and initiative.

Teaching Accountability

Instilling a sense of accountability in your son is paramount for his development into a responsible adult. This begins with making sure he comprehends that every choice he makes is followed by consequences. When he makes a decision that doesn't turn out as expected, it's important not to immediately rectify the situation for him. Instead, guide him through understanding what went wrong and what he can learn from it. In addition, when he faces challenges, resist the urge to provide solutions. Instead, encourage him to think critically, brainstorm, and identify potential solutions on his own. This approach fosters independence and enhances his problem-solving skills, preparing him for the complexities of the world ahead.

Nurturing Independence in Relationships

In cultivating independence within relationships, it's essential to instill the core tenets of interpersonal dynamics in your son. This includes understanding the pivotal role of mutual respect, setting and acknowledging boundaries, and honing effective communication techniques, especially in friendships and potential romantic engagements. Alongside these relational skills, guiding him to value his individuality is equally crucial. Ensure he grasps the importance of preserving his unique identity and maintaining a sense of autonomy, even when deeply entwined in intimate relationships.

By nurturing independence, you're not just preparing your son for the world outside; you're equipping him with the confidence, knowledge, and skills to navigate life's challenges with grace and aplomb. Remember, the aim isn't to create a distance but to empower him to stand tall, make informed choices, and relish the journey of personal growth.

Allow Your Son the Privacy You Would Want

As parents, the urge to be intricately involved in every facet of your children's lives is natural. However, as your son progresses from boyhood to adolescence and beyond, the desire and rightful need for privacy becomes more pronounced. Recognizing this need and respecting it is integral, not only for his personal growth but also for fostering trust and understanding in your relationship.

Understanding Privacy

Everyone has unique boundaries concerning their privacy. This need for personal space can emerge in various ways, from desiring a private room to maintaining a locked diary or carving out moments of solitude. In our modern, digitized era, this concept of personal space has also expanded to include the digital realm. It's essential to respect and understand the boundaries set on online platforms, whether on social media, emails, or private messaging channels.

Respecting Boundaries

Respecting an individual's boundaries builds trust and understanding. Simple gestures, like knocking and waiting for a response before entering his room, can send a powerful message of mutual respect. Similarly, avoid delving into his belongings, diaries, or digital devices without his consent. Rather than resorting to covert methods to gain information, it's more beneficial to foster an atmosphere where he willingly approaches you with his worries and feelings, assured that his concerns will be addressed with empathy and without prejudice. This creates a foundation for open and genuine communication.

Guiding Digital Privacy

Guiding a young individual through the intricacies of digital privacy is paramount in today's interconnected era. Start by teaching him the significance of safeguarding personal information online, making him cognizant of potential risks and the enduring nature of digital imprints. While it's crucial to monitor online engagements, particularly during impressionable teenage years, it's equally vital not to erode the foundation of trust. Avoid accessing his accounts or delving into private chats. Instead, emphasize the importance of open dialogue, ensuring he can navigate the digital realm safely and responsibly.

Appreciating Emotional Privacy

Understand that he might not always be ready to share every emotion or thought. Instead of prodding him to reveal all, emphasize your enduring presence and unwavering support, assuring him you're there to listen whenever he's ready to share. Respect his decisions on sharing relationship details as he navigates adolescence and romantic entanglements. It's about balancing parental guidance and granting him the autonomy to navigate his emotional journey.

Building Trust

To build trust, it's essential to foster an environment that encourages open dialogue, allowing you and your son to address concerns about privacy. This foundation of mutual respect can significantly deepen your trust and understanding. Leading by example and showing respect for his privacy and that of other family members and friends reinforces your value on personal boundaries.

Creating Safe Spaces for Conversation

Building trust starts by creating environments where open dialogue can occur without judgment. This could mean setting aside regular, dedicated time for discussions where both you and your son can express thoughts, feelings, and concerns. A neutral setting often works best — perhaps a calm corner of a room or a quiet outdoor area, away from distractions and interruptions.

Establishing Guidelines for Open Dialogue

To further enhance the quality of conversations, establish some "ground rules" for open dialogue. For example, ensure that both parties are given equal time to speak and listen. Make it clear that it's a judgment-free zone where all feelings are valid and all opinions are respected. Reinforce that the purpose is mutual understanding, not winning an argument or exerting control.

Empowering Them to Speak Up

Encourage your son to express his concerns. Validate these expressions and engage in constructive dialogue to find solutions. If there are nonnegotiable boundaries because of safety or ethical concerns, communicate these clearly and explain the reasons behind them.

By taking these steps, you cultivate a relationship characterized by mutual respect, openness, and a strong foundation of trust. This helps your son to feel secure in coming to you with concerns, questions, or dilemmas he might face, reinforcing a resilient and enduring parent-child bond.

Re-Evaluating Boundaries

As your son matures, his perception of and need for privacy will inevitably shift. It's essential to recognize these changes and regularly converse about adjusting boundaries to accommodate his burgeoning independence. Any inadvertent breach of privacy shouldn't just be brushed under the rug. Instead, treat it as an opportunity for growth. Engage in a discussion, strive to understand each other's viewpoints, and collaboratively find measures to prevent similar incidents in the future.

By granting your son the same privacy you'd expect, you acknowledge his growing independence and empower him to develop a strong sense of self. This autonomy, coupled with knowing that he's trusted and respected, lays the foundation for a relationship deeply rooted in mutual understanding, respect, and unwavering trust.

Offer Additional Support When Needed

Every child, irrespective of being a CD or MY, will face moments of uncertainty, challenges, or emotional turbulence. These periods, often triggered by external events or internal conflicts, require more than just routine guidance. As caregivers, it's crucial to discern these moments and provide that extra layer of support.

Your son might exhibit signs of withdrawal or changes in behavior or voice his concerns directly. In such instances, it's not just about addressing the overt issues but understanding the underlying sentiments. For CDs, this might manifest as prolonged periods of solitude, while MYs might appear overly expressive or even erratic.

A targeted approach is beneficial:

- **Active Listening:** Pay undivided attention, letting him articulate his feelings without interruption.

- **Open Dialogue:** Foster a safe space for sharing, emphasizing that his feelings are valid.

- **Reassurance:** Offer comfort, emphasizing your presence and understanding.

- **Seek External Help:** If challenges persist, consider counseling or therapy as a support avenue.

- **Regular Check-Ins:** Frequent conversations during tough times can provide much-needed stability and assurance.

By being attentive and responsive, you build a robust support system for your son during challenging phases.

Key Takeaways

The journey through this chapter unveils the nuanced strategies and approaches to effective socialization tailored for the distinct personalities of CDs and MYs. It's an intricate dance of understanding, nurturing, and respecting your son's individuality while fostering an environment conducive to his social growth.

- **Respect Individual Needs:** Understand the dichotomy between CDs' preference for solitude and MYs' drive for social interaction. It's about crafting an environment where every nuance feels acknowledged and validated, ensuring your son feels seen.

- **Incorporate Diverse Activities:** Integrate activities that resonate with both CDs and MYs. This approach allows your son to navigate both introspective and interactive realms, enriching his social palette.

- **Strategically Plan Tailored Social Engagements:** Design activities that cater specifically to your son's inherent social tendencies, whether they lean toward the contemplative moments of CDs or the vivacious engagements of MYs.

- **Celebrate the MY's Exuberance:** Recognize and champion the MY's intrinsic zest for broad social connections. By doing so, you provide a nurturing ground for their innate desire to mingle and connect.

- **Set Thoughtful Boundaries:** Implement age-appropriate boundaries that balance safeguarding and granting autonomy, enabling your son to confidently explore his social environment.

- **Champion Peer Connections:** Advocate for the formation and nurturing of friendships. Such relationships are invaluable, acting as catalysts for holistic growth, be it emotional, social, or cognitive.

- **Cherish Collective Family Time:** Dedicate moments where family comes together in shared activities. These instances cultivate unity, infusing the family fabric with cherished memories and a reinforced sense of belonging.

- **Empower Decision-Making and Independence:** Provide opportunities for your son to grapple with decisions and challenges. This strategy fosters self-confidence, bolstering their sense of agency.

- **Respect Privacy:** As much as you treasure your moments of solitude, it's imperative to afford your son his private sanctuaries where he can grow, muse, and crystallize his identity.

- **Offer Support:** Discern times when your son needs that extra bit of emotional or mental support. Be his anchor, offering stability while also granting him the latitude to chart his course.

Remember, socialization isn't just about exposing your son to varied social scenarios but ensuring he navigates them effectively, understanding his unique personality and needs. It's about laying a foundation for him to form meaningful connections, understand societal norms, and grow as a well-rounded individual. By embracing the insights and strategies in this chapter, you set your son on a path to meaningful interactions, genuine friendships, and a deeper understanding of himself and the world around him.

Chapter Five

Get on the Same Wavelength

Navigating the intricacies of emotions, particularly in the dynamic parent-son relationship, demands understanding, empathy, and consistent effort. As we journey further into comprehending CDs and MYs, it becomes clear that while they differ in their emotional expressions, both bring invaluable emotional strengths to the family unit. The aim of this chapter is not just about identifying these strengths but learning to harmonize them, facilitating smoother interactions and deeper connections. By acknowledging and validating these emotional nuances, you can foster an environment of mutual respect and understanding, allowing you to truly get on the same wavelength as your sons.

Celebrate the Emotional Strengths Each Type Brings to the Family

A family thrives when each member's emotional contributions are acknowledged and celebrated. Within this dynamic, individual emotional tendencies collectively shape the family's emotional culture. Recognizing and valuing these distinct contributions fosters a sense of belonging and strengthens familial ties.

CDs possess a natural propensity for introspection, providing the family with depth, stability, and thoughtful perspectives. Their ability to internalize and process experiences offers the family well-considered advice and a calm presence during challenging times. Their inherent tendency to think before acting ensures that their actions are deliberate and informed. By acknowledging and nurturing this introspective nature, you enable CDs to bring their unique insights to the forefront, enriching the family's overall dynamic.

MYs, in contrast, serve as the family's emotional pulse, bringing forth vibrancy, spontaneity, and enthusiasm. They often serve as catalysts for open dialogue because of their willingness to vocalize their feelings and concerns. This forthright approach to communication ensures that emotions are addressed promptly, preventing potential misunderstandings or conflicts. Encouraging MYs to continue being expressive fosters an environment where emotional transparency is the norm, enabling family members to respond promptly to each other's needs.

However, it's crucial to understand that the emotional contributions of CDs and MYs are not in competition. Rather, they function synergistically, each filling roles the other may not naturally gravitate toward. This symbiotic relationship between the two emotional styles provides the family with a balanced and comprehensive emotional toolkit. By emphasizing the unique strengths each type offers, you foster an environment where every son feels validated in his emotional expression. This mutual appreciation and understanding lay the foundation for a resilient and emotionally attuned family unit.

Offer Emotional Support to MYs in Their Social Endeavors and Understand CDs in Their Introspective Moments

Parenting isn't a one-size-fits-all endeavor. Emotional support, often considered the cornerstone of a nurturing parent-child relationship, must be tailored to suit the diverse temperaments and inclinations of your son. Whether you're dealing with an extroverted MY who thrives on social interactions or a contemplative CD who finds comfort in introspection, understanding their unique emotional pathways can deepen your relationship. In the following sections, we delve into specific ways to offer emotional support that resonates with MYs and CDs.

Extending Support to MYs in Social Interactions

Every son, regardless of being an MY, CD, or Straddler, seeks validation, understanding, and reassurance from his family. Their emotional journey and the ways they seek fulfillment and validation differ considerably because of their unique personality traits. To cultivate a profound and genuine connection between parents and sons, it's vital to recognize, appreciate, and cater to these varied emotional pathways.

MY sons are inherently social beings. Their extroverted essence propels them to actively seek out and immerse themselves in diverse social situations. From participating in group activities, starting or engaging in light-hearted banter with peers, to enthusiastically attending spontaneous gatherings, these encounters serve not only as their sources of joy but also as critical anchors for their emotional well-being. These interactions provide them with a sense of belonging, self-worth, and validation.

For parents, comprehending the deep-seated significance of these interactions for MYs is of paramount importance. Offering support extends beyond just permitting attendance at such events. It's about engaging with them, showing genuine interest in their experiences, and offering a safe space for them to share. This could involve setting aside time for daily or weekly chats, actively taking part or showing interest in their social events, or even seeking their perspectives on social dynamics. By doing so, parents can reassure MYs of their irreplaceable and esteemed position within the family and fortify the foundation of mutual trust, understanding, and appreciation.

Valuing Introspection in CDs

CDs often derive emotional comfort, clarity, and rejuvenation from periods of introspection, self-reflection, and solitude. Unlike the extroverted MYs, CDs prefer delving deep into their thoughts, often requiring extended periods to analyze, comprehend, and process their feelings, experiences, and observations.

It's easy for these introspective moments to be misconstrued as aloofness, indifference, or even detachment. However, for CDs, these moments are their way of emotionally recharging, seeking clarity, and achieving inner equilibrium. Recognizing this crucial aspect of their personality is vital for parents. Such acknowledgment can manifest in several tangible actions: granting them undisturbed personal space, allowing for pauses in conversations, or merely being a silent and supportive presence without pressing for immediate responses or reactions. Facilitating an environment where they feel secure in taking their introspective breaks, perhaps by providing them with a quiet personal space or understanding their need to take solo walks, can be immensely beneficial.

The journey of parenting is nuanced and multifaceted. While MYs often seek validation and support in overtly social manners, CDs lean toward subtler, introspective modes of emotional expression and rejuvenation. Recognizing, respecting, and catering to these diverse needs can significantly enhance the emotional rapport between parents and their sons. This approach ensures that each son, with his distinct emotional orientation, feels consistently seen, valued, and understood.

Conflicts Will Arise—Know How to Handle Them

In every family dynamic, especially those that prioritize understanding and open communication, conflicts are an inevitable part of the journey. These disagreements arise from the confluence of varied personality types, differing life perspectives, and the tumultuous journey of adolescence. However, when perceived through the lens of growth, these conflicts can be constructive. They serve as windows into underlying concerns, avenues to deepen mutual understanding, and catalysts to further strengthen familial ties. Embracing conflicts as opportunities rather than mere roadblocks is the first shift in perspective that aids resolution.

Understanding the Core of Conflicts

Diving deep into the nature of conflicts involves recognizing the distinct personalities embroiled in them. An MY, with their characteristic fervor, might openly and intensely communicate their displeasure, often seeking swift resolution. A CD, on the other hand, might prefer distancing themselves initially, delving into introspection before mustering the readiness to converse. Being cognizant of these inherent responses and tailoring conflict-resolution strategies accordingly is pivotal. This might mean allowing a CD the essential breathing room to reflect or immediately engaging in a heartfelt conversation with an MY.

The Power of Active Listening

Active listening extends far beyond the auditory dimension. It engages multiple layers of human interaction—cognitive, emotional, and sometimes even spiritual. When you actively listen, you are not only hearing the words; you also recognize the emotions and the underlying messages encoded within them. You are tuning into what is often unsaid, the tacit knowledge embedded in pauses, tone, or hesitance. The act becomes not just a method of collecting information but an instrument to deepen your connection with your son.

Psychological Mechanisms at Play

From a psychological standpoint, active listening can activate the mirror neuron system—neurons that fire both when you act and when you observe the same action performed by another. This mirroring is essential for emotional understanding and empathy, as it allows you to not just hear but feel what your son is going through. When your mirror neurons are activated, your emotional attunement to your son's experiences is heightened, allowing for a richer, more nuanced interaction.

Active Listening Techniques

Several techniques enhance the effectiveness of active listening. Among them are:

- Paraphrasing: Repeat back what you've heard in your own words. This not only confirms your understanding but shows that you are engaged in the conversation.

- Nonverbal Cues: Use body language such as nodding or maintaining eye contact to show your attentiveness. Sometimes, a nod can communicate understanding more powerfully than words.

- Clarifying Questions: Asking for clarification helps avoid misunderstandings and shows your willingness to understand fully. However, these should be open-ended queries that invite discussion, not interrogative questions that may seem confrontational.

- Reflective Feedback: Offering a reflection of the feelings you've identified can assist your son in naming his emotions, an essential skill in emotional regulation.

Active Listening as a Conflict Resolution Tool

Active listening is indispensable in resolving conflicts. It allows for the identification of nonobvious compromise points by surfacing underlying concerns and unspoken assumptions. It also validates your son's experience, reducing defensiveness and facilitating an openness to alternative perspectives.

Pitfalls of Passive Listening

In contrast, passive listening is purely transactional; it doesn't invite deeper understanding. It lacks the emotional resonance that can turn a heated disagreement into a moment of familial growth. Passive listening can inadvertently relay the message that you are not entirely present, triggering feelings of invalidation or marginalization in your son.

The art of active listening is a skill honed over time. It requires intention, focus, and a genuine desire to understand your son's world from his viewpoint. By mastering this technique, you can turn moments of conflict into opportunities for deepening your relationship, demonstrating respect, and fostering mutual growth.

Pursuing the Path of Compromise

Conflict resolution often hinges on the willingness to find common ground. This entails compromises, adjustments, and occasionally, choosing to agree to disagree. While it's natural to aspire to emerge victorious in a disagreement, it's essential to prioritize the integrity and health of the relationship over the fleeting satisfaction of winning an argument.

Recognizing When to Seek External Help

Sometimes, conflicts within the family may escalate to a point where they're no longer manageable through open communication or mutual understanding alone. At such times, seeking external help in the form of family counseling or mediation can offer valuable perspectives and solutions. Knowing when to take this step is critical for maintaining a harmonious family dynamic. Below are some signs and examples that show external intervention may be beneficial:

- Persistent Communication Breakdown: Despite multiple attempts at resolving issues, conversations consistently devolve into shouting matches, stonewalling, or harmful language. This persistent communication breakdown is a powerful indicator that a neutral third party could help facilitate more productive dialogues.

- Recurring Conflicts: If the same issues reemerge repeatedly without resolution, it might signify deeper, underlying problems that require professional assessment and intervention.

- Emotional or Physical Abuse: Any form of abuse within the family is a critical issue that necessitates immediate professional help, either to protect the victim or to ensure the abuser receives the necessary treatment.

- Elevated Stress Levels Affecting Health: When conflicts contribute to stress levels to the extent that they have a noticeable impact on mental or physical health—such as causing anxiety, depression, or other stress-related ailments—it's a sign to seek help.

- Significant Impact on Other Family Members: Ongoing family disputes can have a collateral impact on other family members, particularly children. External intervention can help prevent long-term emotional damage.

- Unilateral Decision-Making: If family decisions are consistently being made by one individual without consultation or agreement from others, it can create an imbalanced dynamic that may require external evaluation.

- Attempts at Resolution Have Failed: Sometimes, family members might have already attempted to resolve conflicts through open dialogue, compromise, or even previous counseling sessions. If these attempts have failed to produce a lasting resolution, further professional help may be needed.

- Inability to Move Forward: Where family members harbor lingering resentment or mistrust that prevents them from engaging positively with one another, external help can offer ways to break this emotional stalemate.

Seeking external help in the form of family counseling or mediation can equip family members with effective communication tools, strategies, and insights that foster understanding and harmony. However, the decision to seek such help should be made collaboratively, ensuring all family members are open to the process, increasing the likelihood of successful outcomes.

Viewing Conflicts in the Broader Perspective

In the intricate journey of parenting, it's important to remember that conflicts, as daunting as they may seem in the moment, are but fragments in the overarching tapestry of the family's life together. These contentious episodes don't have to be stumbling blocks; rather, they can serve as stepping-stones toward greater understanding and deeper connections.

- Contextualizing Conflicts: First, contextualizing conflicts within the grander scope of your family's existence can be liberating. Rather than seeing each disagreement as a fracture in the relationship, view it as a moment of tension within a long sequence of interactions—many of which are positive, affirming, and nurturing. This reframing can lessen the emotional weight of conflicts, making them easier to navigate and resolve.

- Empathy as a Transformative Tool: Approaching conflicts with genuine empathy can often defuse tensions and lead to more constructive conversations. By putting yourself in your son's shoes, you can better understand his needs, fears, and expectations, thus enabling a more targeted and effective problem-solving approach. This fosters a two-way channel of understanding and ensures that conflicts evolve into opportunities for emotional growth.

- Leveraging Communication Tools: Having effective communication tools at your disposal is crucial. Whether these are techniques you've picked up from books, seminars, or previous counseling sessions, these tools can serve as invaluable aids during conflicts. They facilitate not just the resolution of the issue at hand but also the strengthening of the family's overall communication infrastructure. Over time, these tools can minimize misunderstandings and contribute to a more harmonious household.

- Educational Value of Conflicts: When managed constructively, conflicts can serve as didactic experiences for both parents and children. They can become practical lessons in compromise, mutual respect, and emotional regulation. They offer insights into each other's personalities, helping to foresee and mitigate future disagreements.

- Strengthening Bonds through Resolution: One of the most significant outcomes of effectively managed conflict is the deepening of trust and respect between parent and son. When disagreements are resolved in a fair and empathetic manner, it sends a powerful message that each party's feelings and viewpoints are valued. This can profoundly enhance the emotional bonds within the family, making it more resilient in the face of future challenges.

By seeing conflicts not as isolated incidents but as integral components in the family's evolving narrative, you're better positioned to transform these challenging moments into opportunities for growth and deeper connection. By doing so, you lay the foundation for a relationship characterized by mutual understanding, enduring trust, and unwavering respect.

Recognize and Validate Your Son's Feelings Through Periodic Check-Ins, but Don't Pry

Developing emotional literacy is vital in understanding the intricate web of feelings that every individual, particularly adolescents, experiences. Being emotionally literate allows you, as a parent, to recognize, comprehend, and constructively respond to your son's diverse range of emotions. This emotional literacy doesn't develop overnight; it's cultivated through continuous practice, which periodic check-ins can facilitate.

Check-ins are not random occurrences but should be thoughtfully structured to create an environment of safety and openness. The timing, setting, and even the tone of your voice can significantly affect the outcome. It may be beneficial to schedule these check-ins at a time when both you and your son are free from distractions and stressors.

- Timing: Choose a time when both of you are not preoccupied. Avoid times when he's engrossed in a task or just coming in from an exhausting day.

- Setting: Opt for a neutral or comfortable environment where the focus is solely on the conversation. This could be a quiet room, a park, or even during a car ride.

- Tone: Your vocal tone and body language should indicate genuine interest and openness, avoiding any condescension or impatience.

Tailoring Check-Ins According to Personality Types

Different personality types may require different approaches during check-ins:

- For CDs: A respectful distance can often be more inviting than direct questioning. CDs often prefer to come to you when they're ready, and a simple affirmation that you're available can be enough.

- For MYs: They generally appreciate an immediate platform to express themselves. Offering immediate feedback and validation can be particularly empowering for them.

- For Straddlers: A blended approach might be more appropriate, occasionally giving space and at other times actively inviting conversation.

The Role of Validation

Validation serves multiple psychological functions; it not only acknowledges an emotion but also confirms its legitimacy.

- Immediate Validation: This involves acknowledging feelings as they arise, providing immediate feedback that those feelings matter.

- Deferred Validation: Sometimes, the conversation may require you to ponder before providing feedback. Deferred validation ensures you give a well-thought-out response, emphasizing the importance of what's shared.

Navigating Boundaries without Intrusion

The principle of not prying is crucial when it comes to establishing and respecting boundaries. Being a supportive parent involves a delicate balance between offering a safe space for open dialogue and avoiding undue interference in your son's personal life.

Recognizing Boundaries

Boundaries are not simply physical; they extend into the emotional and psychological realms. Whether it's your son's hesitation to share specific details about his day or his unwillingness to divulge the nuances of a disagreement with a friend, recognizing these cues is vital for maintaining trust.

Signals of Overstepping

When navigating the intricate dynamics of parent-son relationships, it's essential to be aware of the signs that could show you're overstepping boundaries. Such signs can manifest in various ways, and recognizing them early on can preserve the integrity of the relationship. Here are some notable indicators to look out for:

Verbal Cues

- Defensive Responses: If your son becomes defensive or argumentative, it may be an indicator that the conversation has hit a nerve or invaded personal space.

- Short or Clipped Answers: When the responses turn from elaborate to brief or monosyllabic, take it as a sign that you may be probing too much.

- Change of Topic: If he continually steers the conversation away from a particular subject, this might suggest that your son is uncomfortable discussing it.

- Explicit Statements: Sometimes, the sign is as clear as your son saying, "I'd rather not talk about it" or "Can we change the subject?"

Nonverbal Cues

- Closed Body Language: Crossed arms, averted eye contact, or turning away can signal discomfort or a desire to end the conversation.

- Physical Withdrawal: A step back or increase in physical distance could show a feeling of being intruded upon.

- Facial Expressions: Watch for frowns, tightened lips, or furrowed brows, as these can indicate discomfort or displeasure.

- Shifts in Tone or Volume: A change in the tone or volume of voice can be subtle yet telling. For example, a lower volume might show withdrawal, while a sudden loud tone might signal frustration.

- Signs of Distraction: If your son starts looking at his phone, fidgeting, or appearing disengaged, it could be a sign of discomfort or a desire to exit the conversation.

By understanding and recognizing these signs, you can navigate conversations more effectively, ensuring that you respect your son's emotional space while still being involved in their life. Being attuned to these cues can significantly contribute to a more open, honest, and respectful relationship.

Prioritizing Autonomy

Maintaining healthy boundaries involves honoring your son's autonomy. This extends beyond significant life decisions to also include routine and daily choices, such as when and how to share personal experiences or feelings. However, respecting autonomy doesn't mean relinquishing parental oversight. Rather, it represents a balanced approach that combines the child's input with the parent's judgment, enabling a collaborative decision-making process.

Major Life Decisions

- Educational Choices: Start discussions about educational paths and course selections. While the final decision might rest with you, ensure his views are heavily weighed in the decision-making process.

- Career Paths: Offer guidance and resources for career planning, but listen to his preferences and ideas, even if you have the final say.

- Health Choices: When it comes to healthcare decisions, include him in conversations with medical professionals. While you may hold the ultimate decision-making power, his input is invaluable.

Daily Choices

- Personal Space: Set certain guidelines for room organization, attire, or routine, but within those boundaries, let him have a say in how things are arranged or done.

- Social Interactions: Be aware of his friendships and social commitments, providing guidance when necessary but also valuing his input on whom he spends time with.

- Financial Management: Allow him a budget or allowance, but also teach him about saving and spending wisely. Your guidance in this area can be the last word, but his input provides a learning experience.

Emotional and Informational Boundaries

- Conversational Guidelines: Show openness to discussing personal topics, but ask for permission before diving deep. His comfort level in sharing should guide the conversation, even though you may need to assert boundaries.

- Emotional Expression: Provide a safe space for him to voice his feelings while also offering constructive feedback or setting emotional boundaries when necessary.

Activity Choices

- Extracurricular Activities: Encourage him to select activities based on his interests, but within the context of what's workable and appropriate for the family.

- Food Preferences: When planning meals, ask for his input on menu choices, but maintain the right to make the final choices based on nutrition and practicality.

Balancing autonomy means allowing your son's voice to be heard and respected while also acknowledging that some decisions require adult experience and judgment. This balanced approach encourages responsible freedom, teaches compromise, and builds a trusting relationship where both parent and son contribute to the decision-making process.

Open Door, Not Open Book

Convey to your son that while the door is always open for him to share his thoughts and feelings, he is not obligated to be an open book.

The aim is to create a space of availability without enforcing a space of disclosure.

Evolving Nature of Check-Ins

As your son grows, the format, frequency, and nature of these check-ins will need to adapt. Key life transitions such as moving to a new school, facing academic pressures, or navigating relational complexities may necessitate more frequent or in-depth conversations.

Periodic check-ins are instrumental in strengthening the emotional bond between parent and son, provided they are executed thoughtfully and respectfully. Through effective timing, personalization, and appropriate validation, these check-ins serve as foundational pillars in maintaining an empathetic and supportive familial relationship.

Model Emotional Regulation and Effective Communication

Your behavior as a parent is more than just a set of actions; it serves as an integral template for how your son will manage his own emotions and interpersonal communications. Your methodologies in emotional regulation and effective communication become enduring frameworks that he will reference throughout life.

Emotional regulation refers to the ability to manage and respond to an emotional experience in a balanced way. This skill is crucial for mental well-being and successful interactions with others. However, it's essential to understand what emotional regulation is and what it isn't.

What Emotional Regulation Is:

- Awareness: Recognizing one's emotions as they occur

- Understanding: Identifying the triggers that led to the emotional state

- Labeling: Putting a name to the emotion to reduce its intensity

- Expression: Appropriately expressing feelings related to the situation

- Strategy Implementation: Using techniques like deep breathing or taking a break to manage one's emotional state

- Evaluation: Assessing the effectiveness of the chosen strategy

What Emotional Regulation Isn't:

- Suppressing emotions or denying them

- Always appearing calm and collected

- Never crying, getting angry, or showing that you're upset

As the closest role model, you provide your son with firsthand lessons in managing emotions like frustration, disappointment, or excitement. When you take a moment to evaluate your emotional state before responding to a tense situation, you're illustrating the value of contemplative action over hasty reactions.

Understanding emotional regulation helps you teach your child that it's okay to feel emotions, but it's also essential to manage them constructively. It sets the stage for them to develop emotional intelligence, a skill that will serve them well throughout life.

Effective Communication

Effective communication extends beyond expressing oneself clearly; it encompasses the art of active listening and the grace of empathy. These elements collectively nurture an atmosphere of mutual respect and understanding. Your consistent engagement in these practices serves as a real-time tutorial for your son, highlighting their importance.

Tailoring Approaches to Personality Types

- For CDs: Given their introspective nature, CDs often require additional time to process emotions and articulate their viewpoints. Parents should be prepared to offer this time and space without rushing the process. Offering gentle prompts rather than pressing questions can encourage them to share when they're ready.

- For MYs: In contrast, MYs might seek immediate recognition of their feelings because of their extroverted tendencies. Acknowledging their emotions promptly, even if a solution isn't immediately available, can go a long way in making them feel heard and understood.

- For Straddlers: These individuals oscillate between the traits of CDs and MYs and thus require a more adaptive approach. Being flexible and attuned to their current emotional state can help. Sometimes, they'll need immediate acknowledgment, while at other times, they may require space to process their emotions.

By exemplifying these skills, you're setting your son on a trajectory toward emotional intelligence and effective communication in all future relationships. You're not just resolving isolated issues; you're equipping him with indispensable emotional and communicative skills that will enrich his personal and professional life. Your leadership, through example, deeply ingrains these competencies, preparing him for the challenges and opportunities he will face as he grows.

Key Takeaways

Navigating the complexities of syncing emotional wavelengths between parents and their sons can feel like an intricate dance. As you journey through this chapter, the importance of understanding and harmonizing with the unique emotional pulses of CDs, MYs, and even Straddlers becomes clear.

- **Embrace Emotional Strengths:** Celebrate the emotional assets both CDs and MYs bring into the family fold. Understand that these strengths are not just personality traits but valuable contributions to the familial fabric.

- **Extend Tailored Support:** Lend emotional support to MYs in their vibrant social pursuits and be there for CDs during their introspective phases. This dual approach ensures both personality types feel equally valued.

- **Navigate Conflicts with Grace:** Understand that disputes are inevitable. Equip yourself with strategies to handle them, ensuring that the emphasis remains on understanding, not confrontation.

- **Foster Open Communication:** Regularly check in with your son, showing genuine interest in his feelings and experiences. This not only keeps the communication channels open but also makes him feel valued and understood.

- **Lead by Example:** Emphasize the importance of emotional regulation and clear communication by demonstrating them in your interactions. Your behavior sets the benchmark, guiding your son on how to navigate his emotions and articulate his thoughts effectively.

In the dynamic realm of emotions and communication, understanding is the cornerstone. It's not merely about coexisting but harmonizing, ensuring that every beat, whether from a CD, MY, or Straddler, finds its rightful place in the family symphony. By internalizing the insights from this chapter, you're fostering an environment where emotions are recognized, communication is effective, and every member, especially your son, feels validated and cherished.

Chapter Six

Establishing Healthy Boundaries

In the intricate fabric of parent-child relationships, boundaries act as essential threads that help maintain the structure and integrity of the connection. These boundaries are not mere rules or restrictions; rather, they serve as a framework within which mutual respect, understanding, and autonomy flourish. Given that CDs, MYs, and Straddlers have unique emotional and behavioral traits, the boundaries suited for each will naturally vary. The thoughtful establishment and consistent maintenance of these boundaries not only reinforce the parent-child bond but also provide your son with vital skills that will serve him in all future relationships, both personal and professional.

Boundaries operate on multiple levels, from emotional and psychological to physical and time-based. They demarcate personal space, influence how time and resources are shared, and even dictate the rhythm of conversations. Importantly, these boundaries are fluid and require periodic reassessment to align with your son's developmental milestones and emerging individuality.

Create Boundaries *with* Your Son

The process of establishing boundaries is a critical component of both child development and the functioning of family units. These guidelines serve multiple purposes, including the demarcation of acceptable behaviors, the setting of explicit expectations, and the encouragement of healthy independence.

- Understand the Core Purpose of Boundaries: The foundational role of boundaries is to safeguard emotional and physical well-being. They delineate acceptable behaviors and interactions, contributing to a secure environment that supports developmental growth. Understanding this core purpose helps inform the creation of boundaries that are not arbitrary but rooted in safety and respect.

- Engage in Collaborative Decision-Making: Rather than imposing boundaries in a top-down manner, the process should be collaborative, involving the child to an age-appropriate extent. This participatory approach encourages a sense of agency and responsibility in the child while also ensuring that the established boundaries are attuned to his individual needs and developmental stage.

- Ensure Consistent Enforcement: Consistency in the enforcement of boundaries is crucial for their effectiveness. While some degree of flexibility is necessary to accommodate changing circumstances, haphazard or inconsistent application of rules can undermine their efficacy and contribute to uncertainty.

- Maintain Open and Transparent Communication: Open communication is essential in setting and maintaining effective boundaries. Regular discussions that articulate the rationale behind specific boundaries can foster a shared understanding, making it more likely that these boundaries will be respected.

- Set and Uphold Exemplary Standards: Parents play a critical role as models of boundary-setting and -keeping. Demonstrating adherence to both personal and family boundaries reinforces their importance and offers a practical example for the child to emulate.

- Associate Boundaries with Consequences and Rewards: Boundaries gain more traction when they are associated with tangible consequences for violations and rewards for adherence. This creates a feedback loop that positively reinforces compliance while discouraging transgressions.

- Conduct Periodic Re-Evaluations: Given the dynamic nature of child development, periodic reassessment of established boundaries is advisable. As the child matures and his contextual circumstances change—be it social environment, academic pressures, or emotional development—the boundaries may require recalibration to stay relevant and effective.

Boundaries should not be perceived as limitations but as constructs that empower the child to function with assurance and autonomy. They establish a dual role of providing protection while promoting independence and mutual respect. By carefully establishing, communicating, and consistently enforcing these boundaries, parents lay a robust foundation for a functional and respectful parent-child relationship while also imparting important skills for future interpersonal relationships.

Give Your CD Space and Quiet Time

Understanding the distinct needs of sons who are CDs is indispensable for constructing an environment that supports their mental and emotional well-being. One of the hallmark traits of CDs is their requirement for solitude. It's not simply a whim or a casual preference; rather, it serves a very concrete purpose in their lives. Solitude acts as a rejuvenating mechanism, a time when they can quietly process their thoughts, emotions, and the multitude of experiences they've encountered.

It's important to demystify any potential misconceptions regarding the nature of solitude for CDs. Far from being a sign of loneliness or an unhealthy detachment from social activities, solitude should be understood as a self-imposed retreat—a refuge where CDs can refocus, recharge, and engage in deep introspection. This solitude is an active choice, a constructive engagement with the self.

To best serve the needs of your CD son, creating a specific space within your home where solitude can be embraced is highly recommended. This could be as simple as a dedicated corner in his room, filled with items that enhance his sense of peace and facilitate reflection, like books, art supplies, or even calming light fixtures. Alternatively, it could be a different quiet space altogether in the house, away from the hustle and bustle of family life. The aim is to establish an area that functions as a sanctuary, a sacred space that stands in service to his mental and emotional revitalization.

The act of respecting this solitude is not to be understated; it is vital. This means minimizing unnecessary interruptions and permitting him the autonomy to conclude his solitude sessions in his own time. A gesture as simple as a closed door or a "Do Not Disturb" sign can serve as a universal signal for other household members to respect his time and space.

Fostering a culture of open communication around this need is crucial. Your CD son should never feel hesitant about expressing his need for solitude. He should have the confidence to articulate this requirement, secure in the knowledge that his request will be taken seriously and respected by all family members. If there are others in the household—perhaps siblings with contrasting personality types—it would be beneficial to educate them about the CD's specific need for solitude. This level of mutual understanding can mitigate misunderstandings and reduce potential friction among family members.

Balancing solitude with social engagement is equally important. While solitude fulfills a certain need for CDs, they must also be encouraged to take part in social activities and familial interactions. The point is not to swing too far in either direction but to find an equilibrium that respects the intrinsic personality traits of a CD while encouraging a well-rounded social life.

By identifying, accommodating, and respecting the solitude requirements that are so integral to CDs, you're achieving something incredibly profound. You're doing much more than meeting a temporary need; you're affirming and validating a fundamental aspect of their personality and emotional makeup. This results in them feeling deeply understood, valued, and emotionally secure, ultimately laying the groundwork for a trusting and harmonious parent-child relationship.

Indulge in Your MY's Desire for Adventure and Expression

Understanding the characteristics of MYs—children who exhibit extroverted tendencies, a zest for life, and an innate desire for self-expression—is paramount for crafting a family environment where they can not only exist but thrive. The core essence of an MY is their adventurous spirit and intrinsic need for expression, which demand a distinct approach compared to their CD counterparts.

When it comes to their adventurous nature, MYs are seldom content with a static lifestyle. Their exuberance frequently manifests as a quest for new experiences, be they in the form of travel, interactive engagements, or even intellectual pursuits. These children revel in the opportunity to explore unfamiliar terrains, delve into uncharted activities, and befriend people from varied walks of life. It is as though their souls are intrinsically wired to interact dynamically with the world at large.

As caregivers, this adventurous tendency presents an obligation to not merely accommodate but actively encourage these desires. Providing avenues for such engagement is not an optional luxury but a developmental necessity. Consider organizing family outings that allow them to explore the natural world, facilitating involvement in extracurricular activities that tap into their eclectic interests, or being flexible enough to go along with spontaneous plans that crop up at a moment's notice. By doing so, you are nourishing an integral part of their personality, enriching their worldview, and implicitly teaching them valuable skills like adaptability, resilience, and social intelligence.

Parallel to this quest for adventure is an equally significant need for expression. MYs are expressive beings, and their modes of articulation can range from verbal communication to artistic creation to physical activities. These outlets are not mere hobbies but crucial platforms through which they make sense of the world and their place within it. Acknowledging and supporting these forms of self-expression are vital tasks. This can involve giving them undivided attention as they articulate their thoughts and feelings, championing their creative efforts by showcasing their art or attending their performances, or helping them find the right classes or training programs that align with their skills and interests.

Yet, as you indulge these tendencies, one must not overlook the importance of balanced guidance. MYs, with their unbridled enthusiasm, may at times require direction. Your role isn't just to fuel their adventures and expressions but to provide a sense of balance. This involves instilling a nuanced understanding of when it's appropriate to express certain feelings or how to temper their adventurous instincts with a degree of caution and mindfulness. You're tasked with performing a delicate balancing act: being both an anchor and a launching pad, a source of counsel as well as a beacon of encouragement.

Through these efforts, you are not simply tolerating or acknowledging the innate characteristics of an MY. You're cultivating a fertile ground where these traits are considered invaluable assets. The ultimate outcome of this supportive approach is a child who feels deeply understood and authentically confident. They will learn to harness their adventurous spirit and expressive qualities in ways that are not only fulfilling for them but also constructively contribute to their personal development and social interactions, fortifying their self-esteem and equipping them with a robust toolkit for life's many challenges.

Respect Your Son's Needs

A nuanced appreciation of your son's needs is the cornerstone of effective parenting. These needs can be emotional, social, or psychological and are likely influenced by his personality type—whether he identifies as a CD, MY, or Straddler. Recognizing these needs is a first step, but true respect involves validating them irrespective of personal biases or societal norms.

Addressing the Needs of a CD: Quietude as a Resource

For CDs, respect often manifests as the acknowledgment and facilitation of their intrinsic requirement for solitude and introspection. When a CD opts for a quiet corner or seeks alone time, interpreting this as a mere preference or a sign of withdrawal can be counterproductive. Instead, it's essential to understand this as a conscious choice that enhances their well-being. Consequently, a tailored approach for CDs would involve providing spaces and time blocks where they can delve into their thoughts without interruption, thereby serving their inherent need for self-renewal.

Meeting the Needs of an MY: Social Engagement as Fuel

In contrast, MYs thrive on social stimuli, interactions, and external engagements. Their needs for adventure and self-expression aren't frivolous desires but integral aspects of their personality. Stifling these tendencies equates to marginalizing a vital part of who they are, which can result in feelings of repression or inadequacy. Therefore, an MY-focused strategy might include arranging frequent social outings, encouraging participation in group activities, or simply being available for spontaneous conversations that allow them to express their viewpoints freely.

Navigating the Needs of Straddlers: The Art of Balance

Straddlers pose a unique parenting challenge due to their oscillating needs, which may shift from introspective to extroverted from one moment to the next. Tailoring your approach to meet these dynamic needs involves a heightened level of awareness and flexibility. For Straddlers, it's beneficial to provide a variety of opportunities that allow them to shift naturally between their dual tendencies, making it essential to be attuned to their changing moods and preferences.

Fostering a Conducive Environment: Beyond Recognition

While acknowledging each personality type's specific needs is crucial, creating an atmosphere where these can be openly communicated and fulfilled is equally important. This necessitates a holistic approach that combines open dialogue, trust, and adaptability. Practicing active listening, offering nonjudgmental responses, and being willing to adapt your own expectations are all strategies that encourage your son to feel his needs are not just recognized but deeply respected.

Cultivating Emotional and Relational Benefits

When your son's unique needs are met with understanding and respect, the advantages extend beyond immediate emotional relief. It also fortifies his self-worth, enhances his self-confidence, and enriches the parent-child relationship. By implementing an inclusive, adaptive, and nuanced approach, you pave the way for a family dynamic grounded in mutual respect, facilitating an enduring emotional connection that stands the test of time.

Ask before Giving Advice

As parents, the inherent desire to guide your children often propels you into roles that blur the lines between mentorship and imposition. While there's nobility in the intention to impart wisdom, the efficacy of this guidance is intricately linked to how it's dispensed. This is particularly relevant when dealing with sons who are forging their sense of self and independence, especially during adolescence and young adulthood.

The Double-Edged Sword of Advice

Advice can be an illuminating beacon, shedding light on uncertainties and shaping perspectives. However, when unsolicited, even the most well-intended counsel can be construed as intrusive, undermining a son's budding confidence and eclipsing his own judgment. This is a critical consideration, particularly when navigating the unique dynamics posed by different personality types.

Navigating Personality-Specific Reactions

CDs are inherently introspective and often invest considerable time in internal deliberations before seeking external viewpoints. For them, unsolicited advice can come across as overwhelming and may be interpreted as a lack of faith in their decision-making abilities. Conversely, MYs, with their naturally extroverted tendencies, might be more receptive to external input. Nonetheless, they too appreciate the space to digest and apply advice in their own unique ways.

Benefits of Asking First

Adopting a "permission-first" approach to advice can catalyze several positive dynamics in the parent-son relationship:

- Acknowledgment of Autonomy: By asking before advising, you signal an intrinsic respect for your son's ability to navigate life's challenges.

- Promotion of Open Dialogue: This approach creates a conducive environment for candid communication, where your son doesn't feel cornered into immediate problem-solving.

- Trust Reinforcement: Asking before dispensing wisdom amplifies the message that you have faith in his judgment, even when it diverges from your own.

- Facilitation of Empowerment: Offering your son the agency to accept or decline advice empowers him, enriching his skillset in decision-making.

- Bond Fortification: This respectful approach enhances the parent-son bond, rendering it more likely that he will seek your counsel when he genuinely feels it's needed.

The instinctual urge to shepherd your children toward what you perceive as beneficial is potent. Nevertheless, by switching to a model where advice becomes a consensual transaction, you not only show respect but also lay the groundwork for a robust, mutually beneficial relationship. The seemingly simple act of asking before advising turns out to be a complex and powerful tool, fostering an atmosphere rooted in trust, respect, and shared understanding.

Key Takeaways

Navigating the intricacies of boundary-setting, especially considering the diverse temperaments of CDs, MYs, and Straddlers, is a delicate art. This chapter provided insights and strategies tailored to establish effective boundaries that harmonize with each son's unique disposition. Here are the essential directives to remember:

- **Set Clear Boundaries:** Craft boundaries with your son that are well-defined, ensuring mutual understanding and respect.

- **Honor Solitude for CDs:** Recognize and prioritize the need for personal space and quiet moments, allowing CDs to recharge and reflect.

- **Encourage MYs' Adventures:** Feed the innate desire of MYs for exploration and expression, supporting their endeavors and understanding their need for dynamic engagements.

- **Prioritize Respect:** Always approach your son's needs with a sense of reverence, affirming his feelings and individuality.

- **Tread Carefully with Advice:** Before diving into providing guidance, always check with your son if he's open to receiving it, preserving the autonomy of his decision-making.

By integrating these strategies, you're not only strengthening the bond with your son but also laying the foundation for him to develop a sense of self-worth, autonomy, and an understanding of healthy boundaries as he navigates through life.

Chapter Seven

Have Fun

The construct of fun, though often seen as frivolous, plays an indispensable role in fostering the parent-son bond. Engaging in activities tailored to the unique personalities of CDs and MYs not only enhances enjoyment but also bolsters mutual understanding. As this chapter delves into the variances in leisure preferences between CDs and MYs, it offers a roadmap for parents to navigate these distinctions. The emphasis is on striking a balance, ensuring that while the activities cater to the inherent tendencies of CDs or MYs, they also forge deeper familial ties. By judiciously choosing and partaking in these activities, you can cement a foundation built on shared experiences, understanding, and genuine moments of joy. This chapter serves as a guide to celebrating these moments, understanding their profound impact, and harnessing them to further strengthen the parent-son relationship.

Do Quiet Activities with Your CD

For many, the concept of fun often resonates with bustling activities, lively environments, and high-energy interactions. However, CDs often perceive enjoyment through a different lens. Their appreciation for introspection, reflection, and more subdued environments defines their unique approach to fun.

Engaging in quiet activities with your CD son isn't merely about minimizing noise or avoiding boisterous events; it's about delving deep into an ambiance of serenity and profound connection. Consider the experience of working on a detailed jigsaw puzzle together. Each piece meticulously put in its place echoes the CD's thoughtful approach to life. The ambiance, the mutual focus, and the shared joy of completing a section offer an opportunity for bonding with no extensive dialogue.

Reading together is another activity that can deeply resonate with CDs. Whether it's exploring fantasy realms, diving into a science-fiction universe, or unraveling a mystery novel, shared reading sessions offer more than just stories. They present a platform for introspection, understanding, and even discussions about the characters, plots, and underlying themes. It's not just about the words on the pages but the shared emotions, insights, and reflections they invoke.

Nature, with its inherent tranquility, often aligns perfectly with a CD's disposition. Activities like bird-watching, nature walks, or even quietly observing the rhythmic patterns of a serene lake can be immensely fulfilling. These moments in nature, away from the incessant digital world, offer an invaluable opportunity for your CD son to recharge, reconnect, and share his insights with you.

Sketching or painting, even for those not artistically inclined, can be another meaningful activity. The strokes on the canvas or the gradual creation of an image on paper can be therapeutic and revealing. Through such activities, CDs often express feelings, perceptions, or memories they might not verbalize.

It's essential to understand that these quiet activities are not about curbing enthusiasm or avoiding excitement. Instead, they're about embracing and celebrating the unique way CDs perceive and interact with the world. Engaging in these shared moments of tranquility and focus not only strengthens the bond with your CD son but also allows you to explore the vast, intricate, and beautiful world of his thoughts, feelings, and emotions. It's a journey worth taking, one quiet activity at a time.

Encourage Your CD to Spend Time with the Family within Reason

Family interactions form the bedrock of memories, shaping values, norms, and deep-seated bonds. For CDs, these interactions can be both enriching and challenging, given their inclination for solitude and introspection. Thus, when encouraging your CD son to spend time with the family, a nuanced approach that respects his boundaries is pivotal.

CDs often have a refined sense of their personal boundaries. They cherish their alone time and may periodically need to retreat into their quiet spaces for reflection and rejuvenation. It's not an aversion to family time but a means to balance their emotional energies. Recognizing this, it's essential to integrate family activities that allow CDs to be a part of the collective while still honoring their individuality.

One effective approach is to incorporate activities that require shared focus but not necessarily constant verbal interaction. For instance, a family movie or documentary night can be an excellent option. It offers a collective experience, with room for discussions post-viewing, yet doesn't demand continuous interaction.

Dinner conversations can be structured to cater to the CD's reflective nature. Instead of general topics, delving deep into specific subjects or encouraging everyone to share a detailed account of their day can make the conversation more meaningful and engaging for the CD.

It's also beneficial to establish periodic family rituals or traditions, like a monthly board game night or a quarterly weekend getaway. Predictability in these rituals can make the CD more comfortable and willing to take part, knowing well in advance what to expect.

While collective activities are valuable, it's equally crucial to ensure they're not overwhelming in frequency or duration for the CD. It's more about quality than quantity. A two-hour intensive family hiking trip can be more beneficial and memorable than a whole day of sporadic activities that leave the CD drained.

Importantly, always leave room for flexibility. If your CD son expresses a need to skip a particular family event or activity because of his emotional state, respect his decision. It's essential to communicate that while his presence is cherished, his well-being is paramount. Over time, with mutual understanding and respect, the CD will probably find a comfortable rhythm of family interaction that aligns with both his needs and the collective's desires.

Remember, encouraging your CD son to spend time with the family is about understanding his rhythm, honoring his boundaries, and ensuring that the interactions are as enriching for him as they are for the rest of the family.

Do Independent Activities Near Your CD

Engaging in independent activities alongside your CD son provides a unique avenue to foster connection without intruding upon his personal space. This method respects his natural inclination for introspection while still maintaining a sense of closeness.

Being physically present in the same space, even when engrossed in separate activities, can be remarkably comforting for CDs. This shared silence is not about detachment but about a mutual understanding that you can coexist harmoniously without the need for constant interaction. Here, the emphasis is on presence rather than direct engagement.

For instance, you might read a book or work on a hobby in the same room where your CD son is sketching, reading, or studying. The proximity allows for spontaneous interactions, like sharing an interesting excerpt from a book or discussing a concept, but doesn't place an expectation on continuous conversation.

This approach is beneficial during periods when your CD son might be processing deeper emotions or thoughts. He may not be ready to share or articulate these feelings yet, but your nearby presence provides an unspoken reassurance that, should he wish to open up, you're readily available.

Observing without intruding can grant you insights into your son's world. Watching him immerse himself in a task, be it writing, assembling a model, or exploring a software program, can offer glimpses into his passions, challenges, and strategies for problem-solving.

However, it's vital to strike a balance. The intent isn't to monitor but to share a space. Refrain from frequently interrupting his activity or pressing him for updates. Allow the flow of interaction to be organic. If he chooses to engage in conversation, respond, but if he remains immersed in his task, respect his engagement.

Doing independent activities near your CD son is a subtle yet potent method to reinforce familial bonds. It's a gentle reminder that while he might be on his personal journey of introspection, he isn't alone, and the family remains a supportive, understanding backdrop against which his individuality flourishes.

Allow Your CD to Plan What You Do Together

Empowering your CD son to take the lead in planning shared activities can be a significant gesture of trust and validation. It provides an opportunity for him to express his interests and inclinations, ensuring that the time you spend together aligns with his preferences and comfort levels.

CDs, with their introspective nature, often have unique ways of experiencing and engaging with the world around them. By allowing them to dictate the rhythm and content of shared activities, you're showing a willingness to step into their world and view things from their perspective.

For example, your CD son might choose an afternoon at a museum, a quiet hike, or an evening at home experimenting with a new board game. These activities, while possibly less boisterous than those an MY might select, have their own charm and depth. They provide opportunities for meaningful discussions, shared learning experiences, and moments of quiet bonding.

Allowing him to plan also gives him a sense of agency and responsibility. He will appreciate the chance to think about what would be enjoyable for both of you, fostering a greater sense of mutual respect. This also provides a subtle boost to his confidence, knowing that his choices are valued.

However, it's important to approach this with an open mind. While you might have certain reservations or hesitations about his choices—perhaps because of unfamiliarity or personal preferences—it's crucial to prioritize the essence of the experience over the activity itself. The aim is to bond and understand each other better, not necessarily to engage in a favorite activity.

These moments can serve as insightful windows into any evolving interests or passions he might be developing. It's an opportunity for you to learn and grow alongside him, fostering a deeper connection based on mutual understanding and shared experiences.

In summary, by entrusting your CD son with the responsibility of planning shared activities, you not only enrich the quality of your time together but also fortify the trust and understanding that underpins your relationship. It's a gesture that speaks volumes about your respect for his individuality and your eagerness to engage with him on his terms.

Encourage Your MY to Try New Things

The spirited nature of MYs often comes hand-in-hand with a curiosity and zest for life. Their extroverted tendencies mean they're open to exploration and new experiences. Encouraging your MY son to try new things not only aligns with his natural inclinations but also provides ample opportunities for growth, learning, and personal development.

MYs thrive when they're introduced to varied experiences. Whether it's a new sport, a different type of cuisine, a musical instrument, or even a unique cultural event, diversifying their activities can sharpen their adaptability and broaden their perspectives. This breadth of experience can play a pivotal role in shaping their worldview, making them more tolerant, understanding, and well-rounded individuals.

However, while their extroverted nature might imply an innate courage to dive into the unfamiliar, it's essential to recognize that every MY will have his own set of apprehensions and fears. As a parent, your role is to strike a balance—gently nudging them toward new experiences while ensuring they don't feel overwhelmed or pressured.

Provide a safety net of support. If your MY son asks about joining a drama club but is nervous about the first day, offer to drive him there, ensuring he knows you're close by. If he's intrigued by a new sport but hesitant about his skills, maybe play it together in the backyard first, familiarizing him with the basics before he ventures into a more competitive arena.

Celebrating successes, no matter how small, can also serve as a powerful motivator. If your MY son tries a new dish, learns a few chords on a guitar, or even just attempts a new activity, recognizing and applauding his effort can spur him on to explore further. This positive reinforcement can create a feedback loop of curiosity and confidence.

Encouraging new experiences also offers an excellent opportunity for bonding. Sharing a first-time experience, such as trying rock climbing or visiting a particular art exhibit, can lead to shared memories that strengthen your parent-child relationship. It allows for mutual growth, understanding, and a shared narrative that both of you will cherish.

In conclusion, while MYs might naturally gravitate toward novelty, providing them with structured opportunities, a supportive environment, and a balance of encouragement and understanding can maximize their potential for personal growth. Your support will not only help them embrace the vast array of experiences life offers but also ensure they derive deep personal insight and joy from each new venture.

Incorporate Plenty of Social Interaction for Your MY

Social interaction is to MYs what sunlight is to plants—an essential source of nourishment and growth. Given their extroverted nature, MYs naturally seek, enjoy, and thrive in social environments. Facilitating ample social interaction for your MY son can be instrumental in his overall development, fostering not only interpersonal skills but also self-awareness, emotional intelligence, and cognitive growth.

An MY's psyche is interwoven with the threads of social engagement. Regular interactions with peers, family, and even strangers allow them to process emotions, understand diverse viewpoints, and refine their communication skills. It's not just about being sociable; it's about harnessing the immense cognitive and emotional benefits that such engagements offer.

Here are some strategies and considerations for promoting social interaction for your MY son:

- Enroll Your Son in Structured Group Activities: Let him join sports teams, clubs, or hobby classes to ensure regular interactions with peers in an environment conducive to teamwork and shared learning.

- Host Regular Family Gatherings: Understand that family interactions hold weight in an MY's social realm. Organize family outings or get-togethers to cater to your MY son's sociable nature and strengthen familial bonds.

- Maintain an Open-Door Policy: Make your home welcoming for your MY son's friends. This approach will not only feed his extroverted tendencies but also grant you insights into his social circle.

- Encourage Community Engagement: Propel him to take part in community events or volunteer activities. Such interactions introduce him to a broader range of societal engagements, cultivating empathy and a sense of community spirit.

- Instill Digital Responsibility: In this digital age, ensure he appreciates online etiquette and the importance of privacy and recognizes the value of face-to-face interactions.

- Promote Diverse Friendships: Advocate for interactions with peers from various backgrounds, fostering values of tolerance and global awareness.

- Emphasize Balance: Recognize the importance of downtime. While fostering social interactions, ensure he also has moments of introspection and relaxation, preventing overscheduling.

By consciously incorporating social interactions into your MY son's routine, you are not merely catering to his extroverted tendencies. You are laying a foundation for him to build robust interpersonal skills, understand societal norms, and develop a well-rounded personality. The challenge lies in facilitating these interactions in a manner that's both productive and enjoyable, ensuring your son derives maximum benefit from every social engagement.

Embrace Your MY's High-Energy Spirit

The vivacity and vigor inherent to MYs are defining facets of their personality. This high-energy spirit isn't merely a reflection of physical vitality but represents a multifaceted enthusiasm for life, experiences, and connections. Embracing and channeling this energy constructively is crucial not only for the well-being of your MY son but also for harmonizing familial dynamics.

Understanding the Energy Spectrum of MYs

MYs, by nature, exhibit an outward expression of their internal energies. This manifestation often translates to an enthusiasm for activities, a propensity for initiating conversations, or a penchant for immersing themselves in vibrant social scenarios. The key lies in understanding that this energy is an intrinsic part of their psychological makeup.

Strategies for Embracing and Channeling High-Energy

- Provide Constructive Outlets: Offer avenues for him to direct his vitality, whether through sports, dance, arts, music, or theater.

- Establish Routine and Structure: Incorporate a sense of regularity to manage his daily vigor, balancing flexibility with routine to avoid both burnout and excessive unspent energy.

- Introduce Mindful Moments: Acquaint him with mindfulness or brief meditation practices, offering periods of equilibrium amidst his energetic inclinations.

- Acknowledge His Enthusiasm: Value the spirited dynamism he introduces to family life and appreciate the contagious excitement he spreads.

- Grant Autonomy: Empower him to decide how he wishes to use his energy, fostering self-awareness and responsibility.

- Emphasize the Importance of Balance: While celebrating his lively nature, teach the significance of rest for his physical and emotional well-being.

- Adapt Your Environment: Modify the household to accommodate his zealous nature, creating designated spaces for active pursuits and ensuring household harmony.

By embracing the high-energy spirit of your MY son, you're acknowledging and valuing an integral part of his personality. The challenge and the opportunity lie in guiding this energy, ensuring it's expressed in constructive, fulfilling ways that contribute to his overall growth and well-being. Recognizing this attribute and providing avenues for its positive manifestation can fortify your bond with your son and set him on a trajectory of balanced, holistic development.

Play with Your MY—A Lot

The act of playing, often seen as a leisure activity, holds profound significance in the cognitive and emotional development of children. For MYs, play isn't just about recreation; it's a primary mode of expression, interaction, and connection. Given their extroverted nature, MYs derive immense satisfaction and fulfillment from engaging in playful activities, especially when shared with others, including family members. Engaging in play with your MY son can serve multiple purposes, from fostering connection to facilitating learning.

The Multidimensional Role of Play for MYs

- **Emotional Expression:** For MYs, play is often a vehicle for expressing emotions. Whether it's the highs of joy and excitement or navigating feelings of frustration and disappointment, play scenarios offer them a safe space to understand and articulate their emotions.

- **Social Interaction:** Given their extroverted nature, MYs thrive in interactive settings. Playtime, especially group activities or games, provides them an avenue to understand social dynamics, practice turn-taking, and appreciate the nuances of cooperation and competition.

- **Learning through Play:** MYs, with their natural curiosity, often engage in exploratory play. This inclination can be harnessed to introduce new concepts or ideas, making learning an enjoyable, hands-on experience.

Strategies for Engaging in Play with Your MY Son

- **Active Participation:** Merely facilitating play isn't enough. Actively taking part in games or activities not only enhances the fun quotient but also strengthens the bond you share with your son.

- **Variety Is Key:** Given the MY's penchant for novelty and adventure, introduce a mix of games and activities. This could range from board games and puzzles to outdoor sports and interactive video games.

- **Set Aside Dedicated Playtime:** In the hustle of daily routines, ensure that there's dedicated time earmarked for play. This consistency offers your MY son something to look forward to and reinforces the importance of leisure and relaxation.

- **Encourage Role Play:** Role-playing games can be particularly beneficial for MYs. They offer them a platform to understand different perspectives, hone their empathetic abilities, and navigate complex social scenarios in a controlled environment.

- **Adapt and Evolve:** As your MY son grows, his preferences for play will change. Being attuned to these shifts and adapting accordingly ensures that play remains a relevant and cherished activity.

- **Balance Structured and Free Play:** While structured games have their benefits, it's equally crucial to allow for free, unstructured playtime. This freedom fosters creativity and encourages MYs to devise their games, set their rules, and explore the realms of imagination.

Engaging in frequent play with your MY son isn't just about keeping him entertained; it's about diving deep into his world, understanding his perspectives, and forging connections through shared experiences. Playing with your MY son isn't just beneficial for him; it offers parents a unique window into their child's evolving mind and heart. As you navigate the delightful chaos of play, remember that these moments, brimming with laughter, challenges, and discoveries, form the bedrock of memories that will be cherished for a lifetime.

Build a Deeper Connection with Your Son through Fun and Laughter

Fun and laughter, often relegated to the sidelines in the face of daily responsibilities and challenges, hold a transformative power in strengthening the parent-child bond. When shared between a parent and son, these moments of uninhibited joy and amusement lay the groundwork for a deeper, more profound connection.

Engaging in light-hearted activities or sharing humorous anecdotes is not just a mechanism to entertain; it's a pathway to mutual understanding. Through fun, children, be they CDs, MYs, or Straddlers, communicate aspects of their personalities, share their joys, and sometimes even express their worries and fears in a non-threatening manner. Laughter acts as a universal language, bridging gaps and dissolving any lingering barriers of miscommunication or misunderstandings.

Creating an environment at home where fun and laughter are integral components can have far-reaching impacts. Such an atmosphere fosters a sense of security in your son, reassuring him that home is a safe haven where he can be his authentic self without the fear of judgment. When parents actively take part in the fun, it underscores their accessibility and approachability, qualities that encourage open dialogue and mutual trust.

It's essential to remember that the definition of "fun" varies. While an MY might find exhilaration in group activities or adventure-filled outings, a CD could derive equal pleasure from quieter activities like reading together or indulging in a shared hobby. Recognizing and respecting these individual preferences is crucial.

As your son navigates the many challenges of growing up, the bonds solidified through shared moments of fun and laughter will serve as an anchoring force. These experiences, though simple, create a reservoir of positive memories, fortifying the relationship and ensuring that, through thick and thin, the foundation of trust, understanding, and mutual affection remains unshaken.

Make Memories Doing What Your CD or MY Love Most

Creating lasting memories with your son involves understanding and valuing his intrinsic interests and passions. These memories, crafted around activities or experiences that resonate with his core personality, hold a distinctiveness that sets them apart from any generic, familial activity.

For the contemplative CD, such memories might be crafted in the quiet corridors of a library, during a serene nature walk, or while exploring a museum. Their introspective nature means they often find depth and meaning in activities that offer room for reflection. By prioritizing what your CD son loves most, you communicate a profound respect for his interests, which deepens the emotional bond between you two.

In contrast, the vivacious MY finds joy in the hustle and bustle of vibrant environments. Their memories might be best made at gatherings, be it family reunions, festive celebrations, or spontaneous weekend getaways filled with adventure. The laughter and chatter, the stories exchanged, and the new experiences encountered—all become fragments of indelible memories for your MY son.

It's essential to recognize that these moments aren't merely about the activity at hand. It's the undercurrent of shared experience, the mutual respect for each other's interests, and the implicit understanding that each moment is a cherished opportunity to bond that makes them truly memorable.

As a parent, stepping into your son's world by immersing yourself in what he loves most can be an enlightening experience. It offers insights into his evolving personality, dreams, aspirations, and fears. More than anything, by prioritizing activities that align with your son's core interests, you lay the foundation for memories that will be recounted and cherished for a lifetime.

Key Takeaways

This chapter emphasizes the significance of tailored approaches to engaging with your son's individual personality while promoting an environment of fun and learning. Through the myriad activities and interactions detailed in this chapter, you can harness the power of leisure to strengthen the parent-son bond.

- **Tailor Quiet Moments:** Allocate specific times to enjoy serene activities with your CD, understanding that these moments of tranquility resonate deeply with them.

- **Promote Familial Engagement:** Urge your CD son to partake in family activities, but always recognize and respect his boundaries.

- **Practice Proximity:** Engage in your independent pursuits while staying close to your CD, creating a comforting presence without imposing.

- **Empower Decision-Making:** Allow your CD the autonomy to select shared activities, fostering a sense of control and validation.

- **Encourage Exploration:** Motivate your MY to dive into novel experiences, understanding that novelty and variety stimulate them.

- **Boost Social Opportunities:** Ensure that your MY is offered ample opportunities for vibrant social interactions, as these fuel their energetic spirit.

- **Embrace Vivacity:** Celebrate and become a part of the high-energy world of your MY, sharing in their zest for life.

- **Prioritize Play:** Allocate substantial time to play and interact with your MY, realizing that through play, they express, learn, and connect.

- **Deepen Bonds through Joy:** Use the universal languages of fun and laughter to bridge any gaps and build a profound connection with your son.

- **Craft Cherished Memories:** Take time to engage in activities that align perfectly with the interests of your CD or MY, ensuring these moments are remembered fondly.

To conclude, the essence of this chapter underscores the importance of fostering a vibrant environment where fun becomes the catalyst for deeper connections. While CDs and MYs may have varying preferences, the universal truth remains—shared moments of joy and genuine engagement can cultivate lasting memories and an unbreakable bond between parent and son. With the insights and strategies provided here, you're equipped to embark on a joyful journey of connection, tailored perfectly to your son's unique essence.

Chapter Eight

Final Thoughts

In the boundless landscape of human connections, love arises as one of our most profound yet complex experiences. It is far more than fleeting moments of shared joy or the warmth of a comforting embrace; love is a commitment to growth, understanding, and standing stoically together. In these pages, you have embarked on an enlightening expedition through the intricate world of loving a Cave Dweller or Mountain Yeller son. Now, pause to appreciate all you have learned on this odyssey of the heart.

Understanding the Depth of Personality

Every individual is a unique cosmos of thoughts, emotions, and perspectives. Your CD son may find sanctuary in silent spaces, his introspective nature thriving inwardly, while your MY son revels in lively social spheres, expressing himself outwardly with zeal. Though seemingly opposite, these differences can paint a beautiful mosaic when appreciated. Remember our discussions on active listening, appreciating quietude, and offering verbal affirmations? These are not merely guidance strategies. They are passageways to comprehension, empathy, and profound connection. Peeling back the layers to see someone's authentic essence is the pinnacle of understanding.

The Unwavering Commitment of Love

Love is not fleeting; it is steadfast. It is not a single grand gesture but a daily renewal of choice. Recall the tools we discovered together—from reconfirming bonds, planning surprise outings, and seeking family counseling, to prioritizing quality time. These are not just actions but representations of an unwavering commitment to nurture the living, breathing bond you share. Like a flowering plant, love requires daily care and watering to continue blossoming.

The Adaptive Nature of Lasting Love

Change is inevitable, and in familial relationships, it can signify growth, wisdom, and mutual understanding. Consider the dance between CD and MY personalities—their harmony requires flexibility, balance, and adjustment. Our discussions around financial planning and establishing traditions and rituals were about more than checking tasks off a list. They embodied embracing change, adapting together, and finding joy in evolution.

Celebrating Diversity through Unity

There is remarkable splendor in two distinct souls coming together under one roof. The combination of a CD's introspection with an MY's exuberance breeds something uniquely beautiful. Remember our conversations on custom celebrations, trying new hobbies, and revisiting meaningful places? These are not just moments but milestones where differences unite to create harmonious new memories.

The Journey of Personal and Mutual Growth

Growth is the essence of life. In a family, it is the adhesive binding members through time. Reflect on the times you have buoyed your son's ambitions, championed his dreams, or embarked on a quest of mutual understanding. It is about acknowledging that as individuals, and as a family unit, there is always room for progress, adaptation, and cultivation into better versions of oneself.

The Boundless Horizons of Love

The insights covered in these pages are but a glimpse into love's vast and marvelous landscape. Your unique voyage with a CD or MY son brims with its own challenges, joys, and unforgettable moments. While this guide has armed you with knowledge, every new day offers fresh lessons, experiences, and memories to integrate. Use these words as your compass, but let your heart chart the course.

The Continuing Evolution of Your Love Story

As we conclude, remember that your bond with your son is an ever-evolving tale, marked with its unique challenges, triumphs, highs, and lows. The shared moments, lessons learned, and obstacles overcome make this journey distinctly yours. Absorb the insights acquired, treasure every interaction, and look forward with enthusiasm to the myriad experiences yet to unfold. The connection with your son, in all its depth and nuances, is an expedition worth pursuing with all your heart. Progress with understanding, patience, and unyielding commitment.

Appendices

Self-Assessment Questionnaire: Determine if You're a CD, MY, or Straddler

In the quest for self-understanding, recognizing one's intrinsic personality traits plays a crucial role. This self-assessment questionnaire has been carefully designed to help you discern whether you align most closely with the introspective nature of a Cave Dweller (CD), the extroverted inclinations of a Mountain Yeller (MY), or the balanced characteristics of a Straddler. By reflecting on your behaviors, preferences, and reactions in various situations, this tool aims to provide insight into your predominant personality type. Approach each question with honesty and openness, and remember, there's no right or wrong answer—just a deeper understanding of your unique self waiting to be unveiled.

Personality Indicator #1

Circle one answer per question.

1. Have you ever walked in your sleep during your adult life?

YES or NO

2. As a teenager, did you feel comfortable expressing your feelings to one or both of your parents?

YES or NO

3. Do you have a tendency to look directly into a person's eyes when talking to them?

YES or NO

4. Do you feel that most people, when you first meet them, are uncritical of your appearance?

YES or NO

5. In a group situation with people you've just met, would you feel comfortable drawing attention to yourself by initiating a conversation?

YES or NO

6. Do you feel comfortable holding hands or hugging someone you're in a relationship with in front of other people?

YES or NO

7. When someone talks about feeling warm physically, do you begin to feel warm also?

YES or NO

8. Do you tend to tune out when someone is talking to you because you're anxious to come up with your side of the story?

YES or NO

9. Do you feel that you learn better by seeing and/or reading than by hearing?

YES or NO

10. In a new class or company meeting, do you usually feel comfortable asking questions in front of the group?

YES or NO

11. When expressing your ideas, do you find it important to relate all the details leading up to the subject so the other person can understand it completely?

YES or NO

12. Do you enjoy relating to children?

YES or NO

13. Are you comfortable with your body movements when faced with unfamiliar people and circumstances?

YES or NO

14. Do you prefer reading fiction rather than non-fiction?

YES or NO

15. If you were to imagine sucking on a juicy lemon, would your mouth water?

YES or NO

16. Do you feel comfortable receiving a compliment in front of other people?

YES or NO

17. Do you feel that you're a good conversationalist?

YES or NO

18. Do you feel comfortable when complimentary attention is drawn to your physical body?

YES or NO

Personality Indicator # 2

Circle one answer per question.

1. Have you ever awakened in the middle of the night and felt that you could not move your body and/or talk?

YES or NO

2. As a child, did you feel you were more affected by your parents' tone of voice than by what they actually said?

YES or NO

3. If someone you know talks about a fear that you've experienced before, do you have a tendency to re-experience that apprehension or fear?

YES or NO

4. After having an argument with someone, do you tend to dwell on what you could or should have said?

YES or NO

5. Do you tend to occasionally tune out when someone is talking to you and therefore don't hear what's being said because your mind drifts to something totally unrelated?

YES or NO

6. Do you sometimes desire to be complimented for a job well done, but feel embarrassed or uncomfortable when complemented?

YES or NO

7. Do you often fear not being able to carry on a conversation with someone you've just met?

YES or NO

8. Do you feel self-conscious when attention is drawn to your physical body or appearance?

YES or NO

9. If you had a choice, would you rather avoid being around children most of the time?

YES or NO

10. Do you feel uptight in body movements, especially when faced with unfamiliar people or circumstances?

YES or NO

11. Do you prefer reading non-fiction rather than fiction?

YES or NO

12. If someone describes a very bitter taste, do you have difficulty experiencing the physical feeling of that bitter taste?

YES or NO

13. Do you generally feel that you see yourself less favorably than others see you?

YES or NO

14. Do you tend to feel awkward or self-conscious holding hands and/or kissing someone you're in a relationship with, in front of other people?

YES or NO

15. In a new lecture or company meeting, do you usually feel uncomfortable asking questions in front of the group?

YES or NO

16. Do you feel uneasy if someone you've just met looks you directly in the eyes when talking to you, especially if the conversation is about you?

YES or NO

17. In a group situation with people you've just met, would you feel uncomfortable drawing attention to yourself by initiating a conversation?

YES or NO

18. If you're in a relationship or are very close to someone, do you find it difficult or embarrassing to verbalize your love for them?

YES or NO

Personality Indicator Scores

Personality Indicator #1

- Give yourself 10 points for every yes answer for questions one and two.

- Give yourself 5 points for every YES answer for questions three through eighteen.

- Write the total number at the top of #1's questionnaire.

Personality Indicator #2

- Give yourself 10 points for every yes answer for questions one and two.

- Give yourself 5 points for every YES answer for questions three through eighteen.

- Write the total number at the top of #2's questionnaire.

- Combine the total from PI 1 & 2.

Using the Scoring Chart

On the scoring chart, look up the combined score of Personality Indicators 1 & 2 on the HORIZONTAL axis of the chart and circle the number.

- Take the total score of PI #1, locate it on the VERTICAL axis of the chart, and circle the number.

- Draw a horizontal line across the page from the PI 1 score, then draw a vertical line down from the combined score.

- The number in the box where the two lines intersect represents your true, adjusted percentage personality indicator.

- Scores 61 and higher indicate a Mountain Yeller personality type.

- Scores 45 and lower indicate a Cave Dweller personality type.

- Scores 47 to 56 indicate a Straddler personality type.

Cave Dweller Tendencies

- Reserved

- Head ruled

- Controlling

- Wants space and security

- Prefers socializing one-on-one

- Singular focus

- Thinks before reacting

- Prefers showing affection privately

- Distrusts flattery

- Enjoys working alone

- Enjoys individual activities

- Wants alone time

- Dresses for comfort

- Decides after thinking about it

- Speaks literally, to the point

- Infers from what others say

- Feels emotional pain in the mind

- Fears loss of security

Cave Dweller Priorities

- Career/Financial Security

- Hobbies/Children

- Relationships/Family

- Sex/Lovers

Mountain Yeller Tendencies

- Outgoing

- Heart ruled

- Dominating

- Wants connection and touch

- Enjoys socializing in groups

- Movement focused

- Reacts spontaneously

- Comfortable with affection anytime

- Likes reassurance and compliments

- Enjoys working with people

- Enjoys team activities

- Wants to be together as much as possible

- Decides in the moment

- Speaks inferentially—adds story

- Takes literally what others say

- Feels emotional pain in body and mind

- Fears rejection

Mountain Yeller Priorities

- Relationships/Sex

- Family/Children

- Friends/Hobbies

- Career/Financial security

COMBINED SCORE #1 AND #2

SCORE #1	50	55	60	65	70	75	80	85	90	95	100	105	110	115	120	125	130	135	140	145	150	155	160	165	170	175	180	185	190	195	200
100											100	95	91	87	83	80	77	74	71	69	67	65	63	61	59	58	57	56	54	53	51	50
95										100	95	90	86	83	79	76	73	70	68	65	63	61	59	58	56	54	53	51	50	49	46
90									100	95	90	86	82	78	75	72	69	67	64	62	60	58	56	55	53	51	50	48	47	46	45
85								100	94	89	85	81	77	74	71	68	65	63	61	59	57	55	53	52	50	49	47	46	45	44	43
80							100	94	89	84	80	76	73	70	67	64	62	59	57	55	53	52	50	48	47	46	44	43	42	41	40
75						100	94	88	83	79	75	71	68	65	63	60	58	56	54	52	50	48	47	45	44	43	42	41	39	38	38
70					100	93	88	82	78	74	70	67	64	61	59	56	54	52	50	48	47	45	44	42	41	40	39	38	37	36	35
65				100	93	87	81	76	72	68	65	62	59	57	54	52	50	48	46	45	43	42	41	39	38	37	36	35	34	33	33
60			100	92	86	80	75	71	67	63	60	57	55	52	50	48	46	44	43	41	40	39	38	36	35	34	33	32	32	31	30
55		100	99	85	79	73	69	65	61	58	55	52	50	48	46	44	42	41	39	38	37	36	34	33	32	31	31	30	29	28	28
50	100	91	83	77	71	67	63	59	56	53	50	48	45	43	42	40	38	37	36	34	33	32	31	30	29	28	27	26	26	25	25
45	90	82	75	69	64	60	56	53	50	47	45	43	41	39	38	36	35	33	32	31	30	29	28	27	26	25	25	24	24	23	23
40	80	73	67	62	57	53	50	47	44	42	40	38	36	35	33	32	31	30	29	28	27	26	25	24	24	23	22	22	21	21	20
35	70	64	58	54	50	47	44	41	39	37	35	33	32	30	29	28	27	26	25	24	23	23	22	21	21	20	19	19	18	18	18
30	60	55	50	46	43	40	38	35	33	32	30	29	27	26	25	24	23	22	21	21	20	19	19	18	17	17	16	16	16	15	15
25	50	46	42	38	36	33	31	29	28	26	25	24	23	22	21	20	19	19	18	17	17	16	16	15	15	14	14	13	13	13	13
20	40	36	33	31	29	27	25	24	22	21	20	19	18	17	17	16	16	15	14	14	13	13	12	12	11	11	11	11	10	10	10
15	30	27	25	23	21	20	19	18	17	16	15	14	14	13	13	12	12	11	11	10	10	10	9	9	9	8	8	8	8	8	8
10	20	18	17	15	14	13	13	12	11	11	10	10	9	9	8	8	8	7	7	7	7	6	6	6	6	5	5	5	5	5	5
5	10	9	8	8	7	7	6	6	6	5	5	5	5	4	4	4	4	4	4	3	3	3	3	3	3	3	3	3	3	2	2
0	0	0	0	0	0	0	0	0	0	0	0	0	0	0	0	0	0	0	0	0	0	0	0	0	0	0	0	0	0	0	0

About the Author

Dr. Cline lives with her husband, two daughters, two German Shepherds, and two Yorkies in the hills of North Carolina. Her expertise in relationship building has offered her the opportunity to travel around the world as a keynote speaker and international workshop facilitator.

www.ingramcontent.com/pod-product-compliance
Lightning Source LLC
Chambersburg PA
CBHW060350090426
42734CB00011B/2090